The Love Letters

I Never Received

1000 Funny and Inspiring

affirmations to heal a broken heart

SONJA CROSS

ISBN 979-8-9883459-1-6

TABLE OF CONTENTS

INTRODUCTION

Picture this: You've just found yourself in the not-so-exclusive club of heartbreak survivors. Your relationship ship? It hit the proverbial iceberg, and your heart's doing its best Titanic impression. But fear not, because you're about to embark on a journey with the quirkiest and most heartwarming companion - " The Love Letters I Never Received."

This book isn't your typical self-help guide; it's more like a warm, virtual hug from a friend who's been there, done that, and got the emotional scars to prove it. Inside, you'll discover 1,000 affirmations that'll tickle your funny bone and mend your broken heart all at once.

But wait, there's more! Each affirmation is like a tiny emotional Band-Aid, carefully curated to help you navigate the treacherous waters of heartbreak with humor and grace. Whether you're feeling sadder than a drenched cat or angrier than a bird that just stole your sandwich, these affirmations have your back.

Remember that time when you thought you were the only one binge-watching heartbreak shows while downing a gallon of ice cream? Well, surprise! You're not alone. This book is your proof that countless others have weathered this emotional storm and emerged stronger, wiser, and with better Netflix recommendations.

The timeless adage that "time heals all wounds" might sound cliché, but it's true. This book will remind you that healing takes time, and it's okay. The pain will lessen, and you'll soon be back to your fabulous self, ready to conquer the world.

We're going to tap into your superpower, one you might not have realized you had – resilience. This book will show you that you've overcome challenges before, and you're about to do it again with even more style and grace.

But it's not all emotional stuff. "The Love Letters I Never Received" insists that self-care isn't selfish; it's essential. So while you're here, indulge in some me-time. Exercise, savor delicious meals, catch those elusive ZZZs, and, by all means, revisit your forgotten hobbies.

Now, let's talk about your worth. A broken heart might have you questioning it, but guess what? You deserve love and happiness more than you think. This is just a small chapter in your epic novel of life.

Support is like the secret sauce in the recipe for healing. Don't hesitate to lean on your pals, family, or a therapist. Pour your heart out; it's therapeutic.

In the grand finale, we're talking forgiveness. It's like a healing Jedi move. Forgiving both yourself and the one who broke your heart is your path to unshackling the chains of resentment.

And hey, this heartbreak isn't a full stop; it's a comma in the sentence of your life story. You can learn and grow from it. Consider it your crash course in personal growth and self-discovery.

So, my dear friend, the future is looking quite rosy. "The Love Letters I Never Received" wants you to believe in the possibility of finding love and happiness once more. Keep that heart wide open, and get ready for new experiences and relationships that are just around the corner.

Chapter 1

IT'S OKAY TO GRIEVE

"It's okay to grieve a relationship - even your favorite ice cream melts sometimes! ⛄"

"Remember, it's perfectly normal to feel like a mashed potato after a breakup. Embrace your inner spud! 🥔"

"Grieving a relationship is like trying to fold a fitted sheet - it's messy, confusing, and nobody really knows how to do it perfectly! 🛏"

"Just like a rollercoaster, emotions can be wild. So, let those feelings flow, scream if you need to, and enjoy the ride! 📶"

"Grieving a relationship is a bit like dealing with a stubborn WiFi connection - it may take time to reconnect with yourself, and that's okay! 📶"

"If your heartache were a dance move, it would be the 'break-up shuffle.' Let those feet move to the rhythm of your emotions! 🕺💃"

"Think of your emotions as a collection of mismatched socks. Sometimes, you just have to sort through them to find a matching pair! 🧦"

"Grieving is like trying to navigate a corn maze in the dark - you might stumble and get lost, but eventually, you'll find your way out! 🌽🌙"

"Remember, it's okay to ugly cry, sing sad songs in the shower, and eat a whole pizza by yourself. Self-compassion is key! 🍕🤳"

"Grieving a relationship is a bit like a one-star Yelp review - it might not be a great experience, but it's an important part of your story! ⭐"

"Grieving a relationship is like solving a Rubik's Cube blindfolded – confusing at first, but eventually, you'll figure it out! 🧩"

"Remember, you're allowed to wear your heart on your sleeve, but it's okay to switch sleeves when one gets too emotional! 👕💜"

"Grieving a relationship is like trying to fold a fitted sheet – it may seem impossible, but progress is made one corner at a time! 🛏️"

"Feeling sad about a breakup? Just remember, even emojis have a 'tear' option! 😥"

"If life hands you lemons, make lemonade. And if life hands you a breakup, make breakup lemonade! 🥛🧋"

"Grieving is like a messy room – it may look chaotic, but sometimes you find hidden treasures when you clean up! 🧹🔲"

"Think of your emotions as Pokémon – gotta catch 'em all, even the ones that feel like a 'Sad-achu'! ⚡😟"

"Grieving a relationship is like a burrito – it's messy, but once you unwrap it, you'll find the good stuff inside! 🌯"

"Emotions are like spices – sometimes you need a little extra 'salt' in your life to make it flavorful! 🧂"

"Grieving is like trying to find your way through a maze – just remember, dead-ends are part of the journey! 🧩"

"If you're feeling down, just imagine that your sadness is doing the limbo – how low can it go? 🕺🎶"

"It's okay to have a 'pity party' every now and then, but don't forget to invite your sense of humor! 🎉😄"

"Grieving a relationship is like going through a revolving door – you might feel stuck, but eventually, you'll step out into the sunshine! ✺"

"If life gives you rain, find a puddle and make some splashy memories! ☁️🦋"

"Grieving is like taking a detour on the highway of life – you'll still reach your destination, just with a few scenic routes! 🚗🗺️"

"Feeling like a drama llama today? It's okay; llamas have fabulous eyelashes, too! 🦙👁️"

"Grieving is like trying to put together IKEA furniture – frustrating at times, but eventually, it comes together! 🧰🔧"

"Emotions are like ice cream flavors – sometimes, you just need a double scoop of 'Salty Tears'! 🍦😱"

"Remember, even the most majestic waterfalls started with a single drop – your healing journey begins with a single tear! 💧🐌"

"Grieving a relationship is like doing a puzzle with missing pieces – it may not be perfect, but it's still a beautiful picture! 🧩🖼️"

"If your heart was a jukebox, what song would it play during your moments of grief? 🎵📻"

"Think of your feelings as a Netflix series – it's okay to binge-watch them for a while! 📺🏠"

"Grieving a relationship is like making a sandwich – sometimes, you need all the layers to appreciate the flavor! 🍔"

"Feeling emotionally wobbly? Just remember, even penguins slip and slide on their bellies sometimes! 🐧❄️"

"Grieving is like trying to fold a map – nobody really knows how, but you'll get there eventually! 🗺️"

"Emotions are like fireworks – sometimes, they're loud and colorful, but they always fade away! 🎆"

"If your heart were a book, what chapter would you be on in your journey of healing? 📖💔"

"Grieving a relationship is like trying to fit all your feelings into a tiny emoji – sometimes, you need a few extra characters! 😫🎥"

"Just like a superhero, you have the power to turn your heartache into a superpower! 💥💚"

"Grieving is like trying to untangle a bunch of Christmas lights – it's frustrating, but eventually, you'll see the sparkle! 🎇🔔 "

"Feeling like a rollercoaster of emotions? Just remember, even rollercoasters have their ups and downs! 📶 "

"Grieving a relationship is like trying to fold a fitted sheet – it's a skill that no one truly masters! 🛏️🙁 "

"If your heartache were a workout, you'd have biceps of steel by now! 💪💜 "

"Think of your emotions as ingredients – sometimes, you need a pinch of sadness to appreciate the sweetness of joy! 🍴 "

"Grieving is like trying to find the end of a rainbow – it might be elusive, but it's worth the journey! 🌈 "

"Feeling like a broken record? It's okay; even the Beatles had some hits and misses! 🎶🔄 "

"Grieving a relationship is like trying to organize a sock drawer – you might not find all the matches, but your feet will still be warm! 🧦 "

"Remember, even the Mona Lisa has a mysterious smile – your emotions can be just as enigmatic! 😀🎨 "

"Grieving is like trying to solve a crossword puzzle – some clues are tricky, but you'll get there with patience! 📝💀"

"If your heart were a car, it would have a few bumps and scratches, but it's still roadworthy! 🚗💚"

"Grieving a relationship is like trying to fold a fitted sheet – it's okay to ask for help if you can't do it alone! 🛏️👻"

"Feeling like a Picasso painting of emotions? Embrace your abstract side! 🎨😵"

"Think of your emotions as a pizza – sometimes, you need extra cheese to cover up the sadness! 🍕☹️"

"Grieving is like trying to find a needle in a haystack – it may seem impossible, but you'll discover the needle of healing! 🧵"

"Feeling like a melodramatic actor in the play of life? Ham it up and steal the show! 🎭😄"

"Grieving a relationship is like trying to organize a messy closet – it may take time, but you'll find your emotional sweaters! 👔"

"Just like a phoenix, you'll rise from the ashes of heartbreak, but it's okay to be a little 'crispy' for a while! 🔥💧"

"Grieving is like trying to fold a map – it's confusing, and you might end up in unexpected places, but you'll learn from the journey! 🗺️"

"If your heartache were a sitcom, it would be full of plot twists and laugh tracks! 📺😄"

"Remember, even the most complex equations start with simple math – your emotional healing has its own formula! ➕💔"

"Grieving a relationship is like trying to assemble furniture without instructions – it's frustrating, but you'll create something new! 🔧"

"Feeling like a human emoji? 😫 Just remember, even emojis have their moments of drama! 🎭"

"Grieving is like trying to untangle a bunch of earphones – it's a puzzle, but music awaits on the other side! 🎧"

"Think of your emotions as ingredients in a recipe – even tears can add some flavor to the mix! 🍲"

"Grieving a relationship is like trying to find a four-leaf clover – it's rare, but the search is worth it! 🍀"

"Feeling like a puzzle piece without a place to fit? Sometimes, you just need to find the right puzzle! 🧩"

"Grieving is like trying to get the last drop of ketchup from the bottle – it takes patience, but it's rewarding in the end! 🍅"

"If your heartache were a movie, it would have a surprising plot twist and a sequel called 'Happily Ever After'! 🎬💔"

"Remember, even a GPS can get lost sometimes – embrace your inner explorer! 🌐🗺"

"Grieving a relationship is like trying to fold a fitted sheet – nobody has it all figured out, so don't be too hard on yourself! 🛏👻"

"Feeling like a jazz musician improvising with your emotions? Let the music play on! 🎷🎵"

"Grieving is like trying to solve a jigsaw puzzle – the pieces may not always fit perfectly, but you'll see the bigger picture! 🧩"

"Think of your emotions as a recipe for personal growth – sometimes, you need a pinch of sorrow to create a flavorful life! 🍳"

"Grieving a relationship is like trying to find a needle in a haystack – it may seem daunting, but it's a treasure hunt worth pursuing! 🧵"

"Feeling like the star of your own soap opera? Just remember, drama can be entertaining, too! 🎆📺"

"Grieving is like trying to fold a map – you may take a few wrong turns, but the journey is still an adventure! 🗺️🚗"

"If your heartache were a book, it would be a bestseller – full of plot twists and unexpected chapters! 📖💚"

"Remember, even the greatest chefs burn a dish or two – your emotional cooking may have a few 'charred' moments! 🔥🍳"

"Grieving a relationship is like trying to organize a messy closet – it's a step-by-step process, and eventually, you'll find your emotional treasures! 🎁🛍️"

"Just like a phoenix, you'll rise from the ashes of heartbreak, but it's okay to be a little 'toasty' for a while! 🔥🔥"

"Grieving is like trying to fold a fitted sheet – it's a mystery, and even Sherlock Holmes would be puzzled! 🛏️🕵️"

"Feeling like a Picasso painting of emotions? Embrace your abstract side! 🎨🤪"

"Think of your emotions as ingredients – sometimes, you need extra spice to add some flavor to life! 🌶️"

"Grieving is like trying to find a needle in a haystack – it may seem impossible, but it's a quest worth undertaking! "

"Feeling like a melodramatic actor in the play of life? Ham it up and steal the show! 🎭😄"

"Grieving a relationship is like trying to organize a messy closet – it may take time, but you'll find your emotional treasures! 🚪🧳"

"Just like a phoenix, you'll rise from the ashes of heartbreak, but it's okay to be a little 'crispy' for a while! 🔥🦅"

"Grieving is like trying to fold a map – it's confusing, and you might end up in unexpected places, but you'll learn from the journey! 🗺️"

"If your heartache were a sitcom, it would be full of plot twists and laugh tracks! 📺😄"

"Remember, even the most complex equations start with simple math – your emotional healing has its own formula! ➕💜"

"Grieving a relationship is like trying to assemble furniture without instructions – it's frustrating, but you'll create something new! ☐ "

"Feeling like a human emoji? 😫 Just remember, even emojis have their moments of drama! 🎭"

"Grieving is like trying to untangle a bunch of earphones – it's a puzzle, but music awaits on the other side! 🎧"

"Think of your emotions as ingredients in a recipe – even tears can add some flavor to the mix! 🍪"

"Grieving a relationship is like trying to find a four-leaf clover – it's rare, but the search is worth it! 🍀"

"Feeling like a puzzle piece without a place to fit? Sometimes, you just need to find the right puzzle! 🧩"

"Grieving is like trying to get the last drop of ketchup from the bottle – it takes patience, but it's rewarding in the end! 🍅"

"If your heartache were a movie, it would have a surprising plot twist and a sequel called 'Happily Ever After'! 🎬💔"

"Remember, even a GPS can get lost sometimes – embrace your inner explorer! 🌐📖"

"Grieving a relationship is like trying to fold a fitted sheet – nobody has it all figured out, so don't be too hard on yourself! 🛏️👻"

Chapter 2

I'M NOT ALONE

"I am not alone: There are more people who've survived heartbreak than there are grains of sand at the beach! "

"Remember, I am not alone: Even superheroes have sidekicks – and your support squad is just a call away! "

"I am not alone: Like a Wi-Fi signal, love and support are everywhere, and they're just waiting to connect with me! "

"I am not alone: Even the strongest trees in the forest needed a little help from the sunshine and rain to grow tall and proud! "

"I am not alone: Think of your heartache as a pizza – there's plenty to share, and everyone loves a slice of sympathy! "

"I am not alone: Just like a library, the world is full of stories, and many of them are about people who've triumphed over heartbreak! 📚💚"

"I am not alone: Even in the rainiest of days, you can find a rainbow of friends who'll brighten your life! 🌈☁️"

"I am not alone: Like a treasure chest, the world is brimming with precious friendships waiting to be discovered! 🏴💎"

"I am not alone: Even in the darkest night, the stars of empathy twinkle in the sky of humanity! ✨🌑"

"I am not alone: Just like a chorus of singing birds in the morning, there are people out there ready to sing you a song of comfort! 🐦🎶"

"Recognize that many people have weathered storms of the heart and emerged stronger, just like you. ☁️💚"

"In the tapestry of human experiences, your heartbreak is a thread that connects you to countless others. 🧵🌐"

"You're part of a club of resilient hearts, each with its own story of triumph over heartbreak. 💪💚"

17

"Just as a symphony comprises various instruments, your heartbreak is a note in the collective music of healing. "

"Like ingredients in a recipe, there are many flavors of heartbreak, and you're not the only chef adding your unique touch to the mix. 🍪 🤍 "

"In the grand gallery of emotions, your heartbreak is just one painting, and you're not the only artist who's depicted it. 🎨 🤍 "

"Just as a forest houses various creatures, you're part of a diverse community of individuals who've navigated the woods of heartbreak. 🌳 🌳 "

"In the diverse ecosystem of life, there are many species who've adapted to the challenges of heartbreak, and you're one of them. ⚫ "

"Like a quilt with many patches, life is woven from the stories of those who've stitched their hearts back together after heartbreak. 🧵 🤍 "

"In the grand library of life, there are numerous volumes dedicated to the stories of those who've penned their chapters of resilience after heartbreak. 📚 🤍 "

"Just as actors play different roles on the stage, you're one of the many performers who've portrayed the character of a heartbreak survivor. 🎭 🤍 "

"Life is like a movie with a vast cast, and there are numerous actors who've taken on the role of healing from heartbreak. 🎬 🤍 "

"In the realm of exploration, the terrain of heartbreak is well-charted, and you're not the only adventurer mapping your journey. "

"Your heartbreak is like a verse in the poetic anthology of life, and you're not the only poet who's penned verses of resilience. 📜 🤍 "

"Like planets in the cosmos, you're part of a vast universe of individuals who've orbited the challenges of heartbreak. 🪐 "

"In the world of sports, heartbreak is a familiar opponent, and you're one of the many athletes competing in the game of healing. 🏆 🤍 "

"Just as a farm has various crops, you're a part of the community of farmers who've sown the seeds of resilience after the storm of heartbreak. "

"Life is like a stage play, and there are numerous actors who've delivered powerful performances in the drama of heartbreak recovery, including you. 🎭 🖤 "

"In the grand museum of life, there are countless exhibits dedicated to the art of healing from heartbreak, and your story is one of them. 🏛️ 🖤 "

"Like elements in the periodic table, there are many atoms of heartbreak, and you're not the only one forming bonds of recovery. 🐏 🖤 "

"Just as an orchestra has different instruments, you're one of the musicians contributing to the symphony of healing from heartbreak. 🎻 🎶 "

"In the world of photography, you're not the only photographer who's captured the candid moments of resilience in the album of heartbreak. 📷 🖼️ "

"Life is like a journey with various routes, and there are many fellow travelers who've navigated the path of heartbreak recovery alongside you. 🗺️ 🚗 "

"Like flavors in a buffet, there are many tastes of heartbreak, and you're not the only one savoring the bittersweet journey to resilience. 🍽️ 🖤 "

"In the world of architecture, you're not the only builder who's constructed the pillars of strength after the earthquake of heartbreak. 🏛️⚒️"

"Just as a garden has diverse blooms, you're a part of the collective of gardeners who've nurtured the flowers of resilience in the soil of heartbreak. 🌼🌷"

"Life is like a science experiment, and you're one of the many scientists observing the reactions to heartbreak and the emergence of resilience. 🧪⚗️"

"In the world of technology, you're not the only innovator who's designed the apps of healing from heartbreak. 📱🛠️"

"Like colors in a palette, there are many shades of heartbreak, and you're not the only artist painting your canvas of recovery. 🎨💜"

"In the grand library of life, there are numerous volumes dedicated to the stories of those who've penned their chapters of resilience after heartbreak. 📚💜"

"Just as actors play different roles on the stage, you're one of the many performers who've portrayed the character of a heartbreak survivor. 🎭💜"

"Life is like a movie with a vast cast, and there are numerous actors who've taken on the role of healing from heartbreak. "

"In the realm of exploration, the terrain of heartbreak is well-charted, and you're not the only adventurer mapping your journey. 🗺️👤"

"Your heartbreak is like a verse in the poetic anthology of life, and you're not the only poet who's penned verses of resilience. 📜💜"

"Like planets in the cosmos, you're a part of a vast universe of individuals who've orbited the challenges of heartbreak. 🪨🪐"

"In the world of sports, heartbreak is a familiar opponent, and you're one of the many athletes competing in the game of healing. 🏆💜"

"Just as a farm has various crops, you're a part of the community of farmers who've sown the seeds of resilience after the storm of heartbreak. 🌱🌱"

"Life is like a stage play, and there are numerous actors who've delivered powerful performances in the drama of heartbreak recovery, including you. 🎭💜"

"In the grand museum of life, there are countless exhibits dedicated to the art of healing from heartbreak, and your story is one of them. 🏛️ 🤍 "

"Like elements in the periodic table, there are many atoms of heartbreak, and you're not the only one forming bonds of recovery. 🐏 🤍 "

"Just as an orchestra has different instruments, you're one of the musicians contributing to the symphony of healing from heartbreak. 🎻 🎵 "

"In the world of photography, you're not the only photographer who's captured the candid moments of resilience in the album of heartbreak. 📷 🗂️ "

"Life is like a journey with various routes, and there are many fellow travelers who've navigated the path of heartbreak recovery alongside you. 🗺️ 🚗 "

"Like flavors in a buffet, there are many tastes of heartbreak, and you're not the only one savoring the bittersweet journey to resilience. 🍽️ 🤍 "

"In the world of architecture, you're not the only builder who's constructed the pillars of strength after the earthquake of heartbreak. 🏛️ ⛏️ "

"Just as a garden has diverse blooms, you're a part of the collective of gardeners who've nurtured the flowers of resilience in the soil of heartbreak. 🌻🌷"

"Life is like a science experiment, and you're one of the many scientists observing the reactions to heartbreak and the emergence of resilience. 🧪⚗️"

"In the world of technology, you're not the only innovator who's designed the apps of healing from heartbreak. 📱🛠️"

"Like colors in a palette, there are many shades of heartbreak, and you're not the only artist painting your canvas of recovery. 🎨🤍"

"In the grand library of life, there are numerous volumes dedicated to the stories of those who've penned their chapters of resilience after heartbreak. 📚🤍"

"Just as actors play different roles on the stage, you're one of the many performers who've portrayed the character of a heartbreak survivor. 🎭🤍"

"Life is like a movie with a vast cast, and there are numerous actors who've taken on the role of healing from heartbreak. 🎬🤍"

"In the realm of exploration, the terrain of heartbreak is well-charted, and you're not the only adventurer mapping your journey. 🗺️🗿"

"Your heartbreak is like a verse in the poetic anthology of life, and you're not the only poet who's penned verses of resilience. 📜🤍"

"Like planets in the cosmos, you're part of a vast universe of individuals who've orbited the challenges of heartbreak. 🌑🪐"

"In the world of sports, heartbreak is a familiar opponent, and you're one of the many athletes competing in the game of healing. 🏆🤍"

"Just as a farm has various crops, you're a part of the community of farmers who've sown the seeds of resilience after the storm of heartbreak. 🥦🌱"

"Life is like a stage play, and there are numerous actors who've delivered powerful performances in the drama of heartbreak recovery, including you. 🎭🤍"

"In the grand museum of life, there are countless exhibits dedicated to the art of healing from heartbreak, and your story is one of them. 🏛️🤍"

"Like elements in the periodic table, there are many atoms of heartbreak, and you're not the only one forming bonds of recovery. 🐏💙"

"Just as an orchestra has different instruments, you're one of the musicians contributing to the symphony of healing from heartbreak. 🎻🎵"

"In the world of photography, you're not the only photographer who's captured the candid moments of resilience in the album of heartbreak. 📷📑"

"Life is like a journey with various routes, and there are many fellow travelers who've navigated the path of heartbreak recovery alongside you. 🗺️🚗"

"Like flavors in a buffet, there are many tastes of heartbreak, and you're not the only one savoring the bittersweet journey to resilience. 🍽️💙"

"In the world of architecture, you're not the only builder who's constructed the pillars of strength after the earthquake of heartbreak. 🏛️⛏️"

"Just as a garden has diverse blooms, you're a part of the collective of gardeners who've nurtured the flowers of resilience in the soil of heartbreak. 🌼🌷"

"Life is like a science experiment, and you're one of the many scientists observing the reactions to heartbreak and the emergence of resilience. 🖊️🏺"

"In the world of technology, you're not the only innovator who's designed the apps of healing from heartbreak. 📱🛠️"

"Like colors in a palette, there are many shades of heartbreak, and you're not the only artist painting your canvas of recovery. 🎨♡"

"In the grand library of life, there are numerous volumes dedicated to the stories of those who've penned their chapters of resilience after heartbreak. 📚♡"

"Just as actors play different roles on the stage, you're one of the many performers who've portrayed the character of a heartbreak survivor. 🎭♡"

"Life is like a movie with a vast cast, and there are numerous actors who've taken on the role of healing from heartbreak. 🎬♡"

"In the realm of exploration, the terrain of heartbreak is well-charted, and you're not the only adventurer mapping your journey. "

"Your heartbreak is like a verse in the poetic anthology of life, and you're not the only poet who's penned verses of resilience. 📜💚"

"Like planets in the cosmos, you're part of a vast universe of individuals who've orbited the challenges of heartbreak. 🪨🪐"

"In the world of sports, heartbreak is a familiar opponent, and you're one of the many athletes competing in the game of healing. 🏆💚"

"Just as a farm has various crops, you're a part of the community of farmers who've sown the seeds of resilience after the storm of heartbreak. 🌾🌱"

"Life is like a stage play, and there are numerous actors who've delivered powerful performances in the drama of heartbreak recovery, including you. 🎭💚"

"In the grand museum of life, there are countless exhibits dedicated to the art of healing from heartbreak, and your story is one of them. 🏛️💚"

"Like elements in the periodic table, there are many atoms of heartbreak, and you're not the only one forming bonds of recovery. 🐏💚"

Chapter 3

I AM RESILIENT

"Embrace your inner superhero cape – it's not just for laundry day, but for flaunting your amazing resilience! 🧑‍🦱💪"

"Your resilience shines brighter than a disco ball at a 'Dance Like Nobody's Watching' party! 🕺💃"

"Remember, your resilience is so strong that even alarm clocks hit the snooze button when they see you coming! ⏰😴"

"You're as resilient as a rubber duck in a sea of challenges – nothing can sink your spirit! 🦆🌊"

"Your resilience is like a jackpot – you keep hitting it, even when life tries to change the rules! 💰🎰"

"Channel your inner ninja – your resilience is so stealthy, it can sneak past any obstacle! 🥷🗑️"

"You're so resilient that even a GPS says, 'I'm lost, but they've got this!' 🔵📖"

"Think of your resilience as a 'Choose Your Own Adventure' book – no matter the plot twist, you're the hero! 📚🧑"

"You're as tough as a snowflake in a snowball fight – your resilience stands strong in the face of adversity! ❄️🌨️"

"Your resilience is like a 'Game Over' screen that never appears – you keep leveling up in the game of life! 🎮🔝"

"Your resilience is as unshakeable as a Jell-O on a trampoline – it just keeps bouncing back! 🍮🤸"

"You're so resilient that even the Energizer Bunny takes notes on your endless determination! 🐰📱"

"Think of your resilience as the 'Don't Stop Believin'' of life – it plays on repeat, and you keep singing along! 🎤🎵"

"You're as tough as a hiccup in church – your resilience won't let anything disrupt your groove! 🙏💫"

"Your resilience is like a boomerang – it always comes back stronger, no matter how far it's thrown! □ ✖️"

"Embrace your inner MacGyver – your resilience can turn a paperclip into a lifesaver! 🔧🛠️"

"You're so resilient that even Murphy's Law doesn't dare mess with you – it knows better! 🍀🚫"

"Your resilience is the real-life version of 'Rock, Paper, Scissors' – it always wins! ✋✊✌️"

"Think of your resilience as the Swiss Army Knife of life – it's got a tool for every challenge! CH🔪"

"You're as unstoppable as a toddler chasing a puppy – your resilience keeps the pursuit fun and exciting! 👶🐕"

"Your resilience is so bright, it could give the sun a run for its money! 🌞💰"

"Embrace your inner trampoline – you may bounce down, but you always bounce back up higher! 🤸💡"

"You're as persistent as a cat trying to catch a laser pointer – your resilience keeps you on the chase! 🐱💡"

"Your resilience is like a magic trick – it turns setbacks into comebacks with a wave of determination! ☐🎇"

"You're so resilient that even a Rubik's Cube gets jealous of how you solve life's challenges! 🍀😎"

"Think of your resilience as a GPS for success – it recalculates, redirects, and never loses its way! 🌐🚗"

31

"Your resilience is like a phoenix rising from the ashes –
you're always ready for a triumphant return! 🐦🥚"

"You're as strong as duct tape in a DIY project – your
resilience keeps things together, no matter what! 🔧💪"

"Your resilience is the engine that never quits, even when
life throws you a curveball! 🚗🚀"

"You're as tenacious as a squirrel trying to hide an acorn –
your resilience never gives up on its goals! 🐿️🥥"

"Your resilience is so bright, it could outshine a disco ball
on New Year's Eve! 🎉✨"

"Embrace your inner trampoline – life's challenges may
bring you down, but you always spring back up! 🍤✨"

"You're as determined as a kid searching for hidden Easter
eggs – your resilience keeps the hunt exciting! 🥚🧸"

"Your resilience is like a superhero's secret power – it's
always there when you need it most! 🦸💥"

"You're so adaptable that even chameleons take notes on
how to blend in with life's changes! 🦎🌿"

"Think of your resilience as a lighthouse guiding you
through the stormy seas of challenges. 🌊🏭"

"Your resilience is like a well-practiced magician – it turns setbacks into surprises with a wink and a smile! 🎩🐰"

"You're as flexible as a contortionist in the circus of life – your resilience can bend but never break! 🎪🧸"

"Your resilience is like a trusty Swiss watch – it keeps ticking through the ups and downs of life's adventures! ⏰🔔"

"You're as unstoppable as a toddler chasing bubbles – your resilience keeps the pursuit fun and full of wonder! 🫧🏃"

"Your resilience is like a spotlight that shines on you even when life tries to dim the stage! 🎇💡"

"Embrace your inner trampoline – life's challenges may knock you down, but you always bounce back with style! 🐾👤"

"You're as resourceful as a raccoon raiding a trash can – your resilience finds treasures in unexpected places! 🗑️🐼"

"Your resilience is like a puzzle master – it pieces things together, no matter how complex life's challenges may be! 🧩😊"

"You're so persistent that even a Rubik's Cube stands in awe of your problem-solving skills! 🧩😊"

"Think of your resilience as a compass guiding you through the wilderness of life – it always points you in the right direction! 🧭 🏠 "

"Your resilience is like a rocket taking off – it propels you to new heights when you face obstacles! 🚀 ✏️ "

"You're as unbreakable as a bungee cord – your resilience stretches but always springs back stronger! 🧰 🏠 "

"Your resilience is the map that leads you through life's maze, even when the path seems uncertain! 📖 🟡 "

"You're as tenacious as a toddler trying to fit a square peg into a round hole – your resilience keeps you pushing forward! 🟡 😀 "

"Your resilience is like a GPS for life's rollercoaster – it always finds the route to excitement and adventure! 🏙️ 🚗 "

"Embrace your inner trampoline – life's hurdles may bring you down, but you always spring back with a bounce! 🐗 🏠 "

"You're as determined as a cat chasing a laser pointer – your resilience keeps you engaged in the pursuit of your goals! 🐱 💡 "

"Your resilience is like a magic wand – it turns challenges into opportunities with a flick of your determination! ☐ ✨"

"You're so skilled at adaptation that chameleons ask you for advice on blending in with life's changes! 🦎 🌿"

"Think of your resilience as a North Star guiding you through the darkest nights of life's uncertainties. ❄️ 🪙"

"Your resilience is like a top-tier magician – it transforms setbacks into incredible comebacks with a flourish! 🎩 🎉"

"You're as flexible as a yoga guru in the circus of life – your resilience can bend, stretch, and find balance! 🧘 🎪"

"Your resilience is like a Swiss Army knife – it's got a tool for every challenge that comes your way! CH 🔪"

"You're as unstoppable as a child chasing bubbles – your resilience keeps you joyful and curious about life's wonders! "

"Your resilience is like a spotlight that shines on you, even when life tries to dim the stage! ❄️ 💡"

"Embrace your inner trampoline – life's challenges may knock you down, but you always bounce back with style! "

"You're as resourceful as a raccoon raiding a trash can – your resilience finds treasures in unexpected places! 🗑️ 🐼 "

"Your resilience is like a puzzle master – it pieces things together, no matter how complex life's challenges may be! 🧩 🙂 "

"You're so persistent that even a Rubik's Cube stands in awe of your problem-solving skills! 🧩 😊 "

"Think of your resilience as a compass guiding you through the wilderness of life – it always points you in the right direction! 🧭 ⛰️ "

"Your resilience is like a rocket taking off – it propels you to new heights when you face obstacles! 🚀 🖊️ "

"You're as unbreakable as a bungee cord – your resilience stretches but always springs back stronger! 🎆 "

"Your resilience is like a treasure map leading you through the uncharted waters of life's adventures! 🗺️ 🏴 "

"Embrace your inner slinky – life may push you down the stairs, but you'll keep stepping back up! 🌀 🧍 "

"You're as adaptable as a chameleon in the color-changing contest of life – your resilience makes you a master of disguise! 🦎 🎨 "

"Your resilience is like a wind-up toy – no matter how many obstacles wind you down, you keep winding back up! 🧸🔄"

"You're so unshakeable that even earthquakes wonder how you stay grounded during life's tremors! 🌍🏚️"

"Think of your resilience as a trusty umbrella – it shields you from life's rainstorms and keeps you dancing in the downpour! 🎏🧑"

"Your resilience is like a jigsaw puzzle master – it assembles the pieces of chaos into a masterpiece of success! 🧩🎨"

"You're as flexible as a contortionist in the circus of life – your resilience can bend but never break! 🎪🤸"

"Your resilience is like a toolbox – it's always well-equipped to tackle life's challenges with flair! 🧰🧑"

"You're as persistent as a child determined to catch a firefly – your resilience keeps you chasing the brightest moments in life! 🔥👶"

"Your resilience is like a marathon runner's spirit – it keeps you going even when you think you've hit the wall! 🏃🏁"

"Embrace your inner bungee cord – life's leaps of faith may test your limits, but you always bounce back with a thrill! "

"You're as ingenious as a squirrel finding creative ways to reach the birdfeeder – your resilience always discovers new paths to success! 🐿️🦅 "

"Your resilience is like a chess grandmaster – it anticipates life's moves and sets you up for strategic victories! ♟️👑 "

"You're so versatile that even Swiss Army knives consult you for advice on handling life's multifaceted challenges! CH🔪 "

"Think of your resilience as a compass in the wilderness of life – it not only guides you but also helps you blaze new trails! 🧭⛰️ "

"Your resilience is like a phoenix rising from the ashes – it's a symbol of your rebirth after every challenge! 🦅🔥 "

"You're as sturdy as a bridge built to withstand the test of time – your resilience ensures you stand strong in the face of adversity! 🌉🕰️ "

"Your resilience is like a tape dispenser – it sticks with you through life's challenges and keeps everything together! "

Chapter 4

TIME TO HEAL

"Recovery is a marathon, and you're the tortoise in this race! 🐑"

"Patience is the key to feeling better, even if it feels as slow as snail mail. 🐌 ✉️"

"Your body's mending itself, like a self-repairing robot. 🤖"

"Just like toast, you'll pop up better when you're ready. 🍞"

"Wounds may heal with time, but in the meantime, Band-Aids and chocolate are your best friends. 🍫"

"You're a potato on the mend, and that's just fine. 🥔"

"Growing stronger each day, like a bonsai tree in your garden. 🌳"

"Your recovery is improving, just like a slow internet connection eventually speeds up. 🌐"

"Embrace your pace; even snails finish marathons eventually! 🏃🐌"

"Think of it as defrosting a chicken, annoying but necessary for a delicious outcome. 🍗"

"You're nurturing your growth, just like tending to a plant. 🌱"

"Even if it feels slow, progress is progress—like a tortoise sipping coffee. 🐢☕"

"Recovery's like a Netflix show, buffering now, but it'll play smoothly soon. 📺"

"Remember, even grand cathedrals were built brick by brick, and so is your recovery. 🏛"

"Like a rollercoaster, it has ups and downs, but it's always an adventure! 🎢"

"Nurturing your progress, like planting a seed. 🌼"

"Recovery is a bit like brewing tea, best enjoyed with patience. ☕"

"You're simmering, just like a slow cooker, but the result will be worth it! 🍲"

"It's like baking cookies, waiting for that perfect golden-brown finish. 🍪"

"You're aging like fine wine to perfection, each day is a step closer to greatness. 🍷🍶"

"Putting together the pieces, much like a jigsaw puzzle. 🧩"

"Recovery is like charging your phone, a bit slow, but it'll power up soon. 🔋"

"You're crafting a masterpiece, like a painter with their next work of art. 🎨"

"Blossoming like a garden, as the seeds of recovery sprout and bloom. 🌼"

"Think of it like a stew, simmering slowly until it's just right. 🍲"

"It's like waiting for the rain to stop, even though it might feel like a never-ending storm. ⛈"

"Your progress is as steady as a sloth's daily routine. 🦥"

"Recovery is like building a sandcastle—slow and steady, but oh-so-impressive in the end. 🏖"

"You're mending like a tailor with infinite patience, sewing the pieces back together. ⬜ "

"You're a masterpiece in progress, like a sculptor crafting a work of art. 🗿 "

"Think of your recovery like cooking a meal—each step is essential for the perfect dish. 🍴 "

"Like a snail crossing the finish line, progress is progress, no matter how slow. 🚩🐌 "

"Recovery is like a blooming flower; it takes time, care, and plenty of sunlight. 🌸 "

"Your journey to better days is like a movie, slow-paced but with a happy ending. 🎬 "

"Even the mightiest oak tree started as an acorn. You're growing, too. 🌳 "

"Recovery is like a garden; you plant the seeds, nurture them, and watch them flourish. 🌱🌼 "

"Just like a coffee percolator, your recovery might take a bit to brew, but it's worth the wait. ☕ "

"You're building your own epic story, brick by brick, just like an architect. 🏗 "

"Your journey is like planting flowers; they need time to bloom, but the result is worth the wait. 🌼"

"Recovery is a bit like waiting for a train—you're on the platform, and it'll arrive when it's ready. 🚂"

"You're mending, one stitch at a time, just like a dedicated seamstress. 🧵"

"Think of your progress like a recipe; it takes time to create something delicious. 🍪"

"Recovery is like aging wine; it gets better with time and patience. 🍷"

"You're a bit like a snail, steadily making progress at your own pace. 🐌"

"Just like a watch, your healing process may tick slowly, but it's moving forward. ⌚"

"Recovery is like building a house; each brick matters, and you're the architect. 🏠"

"You're like a baker crafting the perfect cake—each layer takes time to create something sweet. 🍰"

"Just like a painter with their canvas, you're creating your masterpiece, one brushstroke at a time. 🎨"

"Recovery is a bit like gardening; it takes time and care to watch the flowers bloom. 🌷"

"You're like a potter molding clay into a beautiful sculpture, shaping your future with patience. 🏺"

"Just like a traffic light, your progress may be slow, but you're moving forward, step by step. 🚦"

"Recovery is like making a stew; it's the simmering that brings out the best flavors. 🍲"

"Your journey is like planting a tree; it starts with a small seed and grows into something majestic. 🌳"

"You're evolving, much like a butterfly emerging from its chrysalis, beautifully and in your own time. 🦋"

"Recovery is like waiting for a book to arrive; you're eager to turn the page, but it takes time. 📚"

"You're healing with the precision of a watchmaker, carefully adjusting each gear until you're running smoothly. "

"Just like an architect designing a skyscraper, your progress is intricate and takes time. 🏙️"

"Recovery is like brewing coffee; it takes a bit to reach that perfect flavor, but it's worth the wait. ☕"

"You're constructing your own masterpiece, like a sculptor shaping a block of marble. 🗿"

"Your journey is like waiting for a train; you have your ticket, and the destination is worth the wait. 🎫"

"You're like a chef in the kitchen, whipping up a delightful dish of progress, one ingredient at a time. 🍳"

"Recovery is like painting a picture; it takes time, precision, and a vision of the finished product. 🎨"

"Just like a gardener tending to their plants, you're nurturing your growth, day by day. 🌻"

"You're sculpting your future, just like a potter shaping clay into a beautiful vase. 🏺"

"Recovery is like waiting for a red light to turn green; it's just a temporary pause before you're back on your journey. 🚦"

"You're like a slow-cooking crockpot, preparing something wonderful with patience. 🍲"

"Your progress is like a fine wine aging gracefully, getting better with each passing day. 🍷"

"Just like a librarian organizing books, you're putting your thoughts and emotions in order, one page at a time. 📚"

"You're crafting your future, much like a blacksmith forging a masterpiece from raw metal. ⚒️"

"Recovery is like planting a garden; it takes time for the seeds to sprout and grow into beautiful flowers. 🌷"

"You're molding your destiny, like a potter shaping clay into a beautiful vase. 🏺"

"Just like a traffic light, your progress may feel slow, but you'll eventually get the green light to move forward. 🚦"

"Recovery is like baking a cake; it takes time, patience, and a sprinkle of hope to create something sweet. 🎂"

"You're painting your masterpiece, much like an artist adding brushstrokes to a blank canvas. 🎨"

"Think of your journey as gardening; it requires nurturing and time to see the flowers bloom. 🌷"

"You're like a blacksmith forging a masterpiece from raw metal, crafting your future with precision and patience. ⚒️"

"Recovery is like waiting for a rainbow after a storm; it may take time, but the colors will shine brightly in the end. 🌈"

"You're shaping your destiny, like a potter molding clay into a work of art. 🏺"

"Just like an elevator, your progress may seem slow, but it's taking you to a better place, one floor at a time. 🛗"

"Recovery is like cooking a stew; it's the slow simmering that brings out the best flavors. 🥘"

"You're planting the seeds of your future, just like a gardener tending to a beautiful garden. 🌱🌼"

"You're sculpting your destiny, much like a sculptor chiseling away at a block of stone. 🗿"

"Recovery is like waiting for a sunset; it might take time, but the view will be worth it. 🌅"

"You're crafting your future, like a potter molding clay into a unique piece of art. 🏺"

"Just like a turtle, your progress may be slow, but you're moving forward, one step at a time. 🐢"

"Recovery is like building a skyscraper; it takes time, precision, and a solid foundation. 🏢"

"You're brewing progress like a cup of coffee, one drop at a time, until it's just right. 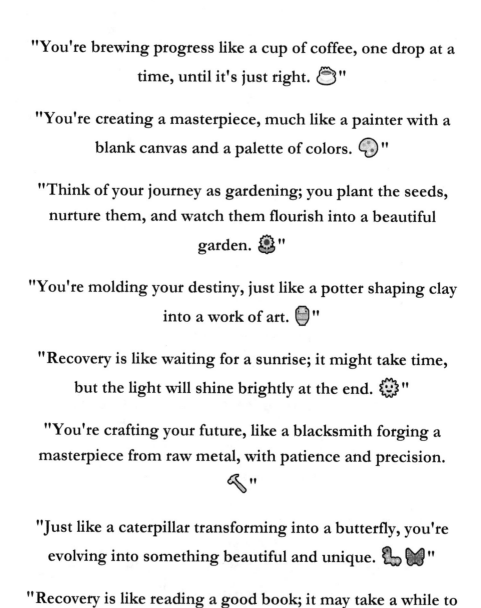"

"You're creating a masterpiece, much like a painter with a blank canvas and a palette of colors. "

"Think of your journey as gardening; you plant the seeds, nurture them, and watch them flourish into a beautiful garden. "

"You're molding your destiny, just like a potter shaping clay into a work of art. "

"Recovery is like waiting for a sunrise; it might take time, but the light will shine brightly at the end. "

"You're crafting your future, like a blacksmith forging a masterpiece from raw metal, with patience and precision. "

"Just like a caterpillar transforming into a butterfly, you're evolving into something beautiful and unique. "

"Recovery is like reading a good book; it may take a while to finish, but the ending is always worth it. "

"You're nurturing progress, much like a gardener tending to their beloved plants. "

"You're sculpting your destiny, like a potter molding clay into a unique and beautiful work of art. 🏺"

"Just like a traffic signal, your progress may have its stops, but the green light to move forward is just around the corner. 🚦"

"Recovery is like simmering a stew; it may take time, but the flavors become richer and more delicious. 🍲"

"You're planting the seeds of your future, just like a gardener nurturing a blossoming garden. 🌱🌸"

"You're shaping your destiny, like a sculptor chiseling away at a block of stone, creating a masterpiece with patience and determination. 🗿"

Chapter 5

SELF-CARE IS ESSENTIAL

"Self-care is the ultimate power-up button for your body and mind. ⚡💪"

"Think of self-care as your daily 'You Time' appointment with life's spa. 🧖✨"

"Balancing self-care is like juggling flaming marshmallows – it's essential and entertaining! 🔥🤹"

"Self-care is your personal 'Life Maintenance Mode.' Activate it often! 🕹️👾"

"Just as Wi-Fi is essential for your devices, self-care is essential for your well-being. 📶😄"

"Your self-care is like a magical wand – it can transform a grumpy day into pure magic! □ ✨"

"Self-care is the secret sauce that makes life's challenges taste like victory. 🍔🏆"

"Treat self-care like the superhero costume you wear every day – it helps you conquer the world! 🧑 🌍 "

"Prioritizing self-care is like a daily dose of happiness. Don't forget to take it! 💊 😃 "

"Imagine self-care as the treasure chest where you collect moments of joy and relaxation. 🏴 🗝 "

"Self-care is like a cozy hug for your soul. 🤗 💚 "

"Think of self-care as the 'Ctrl+Alt+Delete' of life – it refreshes your system and clears the glitches! 🖥 🔄 "

"Self-care is the 'Exclamation Point' to your daily self-love story! 💙 🎉 "

"Balancing self-care is like a tightrope walk, but with a safety net made of good vibes! 🎪 💆 "

"Self-care is your daily 'Mission Possible.' Get ready to accept it, Agent You! 🕶 🕵 "

"Just as batteries are essential for your gadgets, self-care is essential for your energy. 🔋 💥 "

"Your self-care is like the ultimate cheat code – it unlocks hidden levels of happiness! 🎮 🔒 "

"Self-care is the GPS guiding you to 'Happiness Street' – take the scenic route! 🗺️ 🌻"

"Treat self-care like your daily 'Pick-Me-Up Potion' – it's the magic elixir of your well-being. 🪄 💥"

"Imagine self-care as the 'Epic Soundtrack' to your life's blockbuster movie. 🎬 🎵"

"Self-care is like a cozy blanket for your soul on a chilly day. 🛏️ 📋"

"Think of self-care as the 'Undo' button in the grand design of life – it lets you start fresh! ↩️ 🎋"

"Self-care is the 'Pause' button in life's playlist – take a moment to enjoy your favorite tunes! ⏸️ 🎵"

"Balancing self-care is like finding the perfect avocado – it's an art that's worth it! 🥑 🎨"

"Self-care is your daily 'Choose Your Adventure' book – it's your story, so make it amazing! 📚 🧍"

"Just as 'Home' is your favorite destination, self-care is your favorite journey to well-being. 🏠 🌼"

"Your self-care is like a mini-vacation for your soul – no passport required! 🛫 🌴"

"Self-care is the 'Smile Button' that brightens your daily interactions. 😄🫂"

"Prioritizing self-care is like a daily 'Life Hack' – it makes every day a little easier! 💡💼"

"Imagine self-care as the 'Highlight Reel' of your life – showcase the moments that make you proud! 📽️🎆"

"Self-care is like a 'Random Act of Kindness' to yourself – spread it generously! 🫂💜"

"Think of self-care as the 'Rewrite' option for your life's script – make it an Oscar-worthy performance! 🎬🏆"

"Self-care is the 'Chill Mode' for your daily hustle. Sit back and relax! 😎🍸"

"Balancing self-care is like the perfect cup of tea – it's warm, soothing, and just what you need! 🍵🍪"

"Self-care is your daily 'Plot Twist' – make sure it's a good one! 📖🎉"

"Just as a smile is universal, self-care is essential in every language. 🙂🌐"

"Your self-care is like a well-stocked 'Toolbox' – it helps you fix anything that's out of balance! 💼🔧"

"Self-care is the 'Master Key' that unlocks the doors to your happiness. 🔑🏠"

"Treat self-care like your 'Daily Miracle' – it's the magic touch to your life! ⬜🌀"

"Imagine self-care as the 'Enthusiasm' button – it turns the ordinary into extraordinary! 🎉😄"

"Self-care is like a 'Peace Treaty' between your heart and your hectic life. 🕊️💜"

"Think of self-care as the 'Refresh' button in your browser of life – it clears away the clutter! 🔄🌐"

"Self-care is the 'Sunshine' for your daily forecast. It brightens even the cloudiest days! ☀️🌥️"

"Balancing self-care is like the secret ingredient in a recipe – it makes everything taste better! 🥄🍞"

"Self-care is your daily 'Story Mode' – make it epic! 📖🏹"

"Just as a hug is a universal language, self-care is a universal necessity. 😊🌍"

"Your self-care is like a 'Wish-Granting Genie' – use it wisely, and your dreams will come true! 🧞💫"

"Self-care is the 'Magic Touch' in your life's grand painting – add some color and make it beautiful! 🎨🖼️"

"Treat self-care like your daily 'Feel-Good Recipe' – it's the secret ingredient to your happiness! 🍪👍"

"Imagine self-care as the 'Elevator' to your well-being – it takes you to new heights of happiness! 🎰✨"

"Self-care is like a 'Daily Toast' to your well-being – raise your glass to happiness! 🥂🍾"

"Think of self-care as the 'Skip Ad' button in the movie of life – fast forward to the good stuff! ⏭️🏠"

"Self-care is the 'Firework Show' in your daily sky – make it sparkle with joy! 🎆🥚"

"Balancing self-care is like a tightrope walk on the path to happiness – enjoy the view! ⛺🖼️"

"Self-care is your daily 'Power-Up Mushroom' – collect it and face each day with extra strength! 🍄💥"

"Just as laughter is a universal currency, self-care is the key to your emotional bank! 😄💰"

"Your self-care is like a 'Time Machine' – it takes you to moments of peace and relaxation! 🕧🧳"

"Self-care is the 'Painter's Palette' for your daily life – choose vibrant colors and create a masterpiece! 🎨 🖼️ "

"Treat self-care like your daily 'Wish Fountain' – toss in your dreams and let the magic happen! 🪙 🙏 "

"Imagine self-care as the 'Peaceful Oasis' in your daily desert – take a moment to recharge! 🏕️ 🌴 "

"Self-care is like a 'Daily Dessert' for your soul – savor it with delight! 🍮 🍰 "

"Think of self-care as the 'Instant Replay' button in life – relive your favorite moments over and over! 🔁 🎞️ "

"Self-care is the 'Beach Getaway' in your daily routine – relax and let the waves of well-being wash over you! 🏖️ 🌊 "

"Balancing self-care is like a dance – let the rhythm of relaxation lead your steps! 💃 🕺 "

"Self-care is your daily 'Superhero Suit' – it empowers you to conquer challenges with style! 🦸 💥 "

"Just as music is a universal language, self-care is a universal melody – make it a harmonious tune! 🎶 🎵 "

"Your self-care is like a 'Happy Hour' for your heart and mind – cheers to joy and relaxation! 🍸 🍷 "

"Self-care is the 'Pot of Gold' at the end of your daily rainbow – it's your treasure of well-being! 🌈🎆"

"Treat self-care like your daily 'Chocolate Fix' – indulge in sweet moments of relaxation! 🍫🍪"

"Imagine self-care as the 'Hiking Trail' of your well-being – explore it and enjoy the scenic views! ⛰️🏞️"

"Self-care is like a 'Garden of Happiness' – tend to it daily, and watch joy bloom! 💮🏵️"

"Think of self-care as the 'Clear Cache' button for your mind – refresh your thoughts and enjoy mental space! ☁️🔘"

"Self-care is the 'Rainbow Bridge' to your daily happiness – cross it and find peace! 🌉🌈"

"Balancing self-care is like the secret recipe for a gourmet meal – create a life that's deliciously happy! 🍽️🍷"

"Self-care is your daily 'Lifesaver' – keep it close and let it buoy your spirits! 🛟🛟"

"Just as love is a universal emotion, self-care is a universal act of self-love. ♥️🔴"

"Your self-care is like a 'Golden Ticket' – it opens doors to moments of joy and well-being! 📋 🏰 "

"Self-care is the 'Composer's Baton' for your daily symphony – create a masterpiece of happiness! 🎼 ✨ "

"Treat self-care like your daily 'Wish-Bone' – pull it, make a wish, and let happiness come true! 🦴 ✨ "

"Imagine self-care as the 'Daily Diary' of your well-being – write happy moments on every page! 📖 ✏️ "

"Self-care is like a 'Warm Hug' for your soul – wrap yourself in it daily! 🤗 💚 "

"Think of self-care as the 'Escape' button in life's maze – find your way to moments of relaxation! 🔘 🏔️ "

"Self-care is the 'Sunrise' for your daily horizon – it promises a new day of possibilities! 🌅 ✨ "

"Balancing self-care is like a tightrope walk on the path to happiness – enjoy the view! 🎪 🖼️ "

"Self-care is your daily 'Power-Up Mushroom' – collect it and face each day with extra strength! 🍄 ✴️ "

"Just as laughter is a universal currency, self-care is the key to your emotional bank! 😂 💰 "

"Your self-care is like a 'Time Machine' – it takes you to moments of peace and relaxation! 🕰️ 🏠 "

"Self-care is the 'Painter's Palette' for your daily life – choose vibrant colors and create a masterpiece! 🎨 🖼️ "

"Treat self-care like your daily 'Wish Fountain' – toss in your dreams and let the magic happen! 🌀

Chapter 6

I DESERVE LOVE
AND HAPPINESS

"Your worth is like a rare gem – priceless and coveted by those who see its value! 🔷 🩶 "

"Think of your heart as a pizza – it deserves all the love and happiness, with extra cheese of course! 🍕 🧀 "

"Remember, your heart is like a WiFi signal – it connects you to the love and happiness you deserve! 📶 🩶 "

"Just as a cat deserves all the pets, you deserve all the love and happiness! 🐱 🩶 "

"Your worth is like a donut – it has no hole, only sweetness and love! 🍩 🩶 "

"You deserve love and happiness as much as a penguin deserves a belly slide in the snow! 🐧 ❄️ "

"Your heart is like a treasure chest filled with love and happiness – keep it open and share the riches! 🏴 💰"

"Think of your worth as a comfy couch – you deserve all the cozy moments of love and happiness! 🛋 🤍"

"You're as deserving of love and happiness as a dog is of belly rubs and treats! 🐶 🐾"

"Your heart is like a magnet for love and happiness – it attracts all the good vibes! 🧲 🤍"

"Your worth is like a bouquet of flowers – beautiful, fragrant, and deserving of admiration! 💐 🤍"

"Just as ice cream deserves sprinkles, you deserve love and happiness in every flavor! 🍦 🍧"

"Think of your heart as a sunshine generator – it radiates warmth and attracts love and happiness like sunflowers! 🌼 🌻"

"Your worth is like a superhero's cape – it's a symbol of your strength and deserving of love and happiness! 🦸 🤍"

"You're as deserving of love and happiness as a koala is of eucalyptus leaves and cuddles! 🐨 🌿"

"Your heart is like a jukebox – play all the love songs and dance to the rhythm of happiness! 🎶 ♥"

"You deserve love and happiness as much as a dolphin deserves to swim freely in the ocean! 🐬 🌊"

"Think of your worth as a rainbow – it shines brightly, reminding you of your deserving love and happiness! ♥"

"Your worth is like a cozy blanket – it wraps you in comfort and deserving of all the warmth of love and happiness! 🛏 ♥"

"You're as deserving of love and happiness as a squirrel is of acorns and treehouse adventures! 🐿 🌳"

"Your heart is like a festival – celebrate it with love and happiness like confetti! 🎉 ♥"

"Think of your worth as a delicious meal – you're deserving of all the flavors and spices of love and happiness! 🥝 🌙"

"Your worth is like a rainbow – a beautiful reminder that you're deserving of love and happiness every day! 🌈 ♥"

"You deserve love and happiness as much as a giraffe deserves a good view and plenty of snacks! 🦒 🌿"

"Your heart is like a shooting star – make a wish for love and happiness, and watch it come true! ✏️🤍"

"You're as deserving of love and happiness as a meerkat is of a lookout point and family support! 🗿👀"

"Your worth is like a warm cup of cocoa – it's comforting and deserving of all the marshmallows of love and happiness! ☕🤍"

"Think of your heart as a book of adventures – each page is deserving of a new chapter filled with love and happiness! 📖🤍"

"Your worth is like a starry night – you shine brightly and are deserving of love and happiness as endless as the sky! 🌑🤍"

"You deserve love and happiness as much as a fox deserves a cozy den and a clever plan! 🦊🏠"

"Your heart is like a treasure map – follow it to find the X that marks the spot of love and happiness! 🗺️🤍"

"Think of your worth as a cozy campfire – deserving of all the stories and s'mores of love and happiness! 🔥🤍"

"Your worth is like a ray of sunshine – it brightens your path and is deserving of all the warmth of love and happiness! ✹ 🖤 "

"You're as deserving of love and happiness as a sea otter is of a comfy kelp bed and a playful float! 🦦🌿 "

"Your heart is like a magical wand – use it to create moments of love and happiness in your life! ☐ 🖤 "

"Your worth is like a star in the night sky – unique and deserving of all the wishes for love and happiness! 🪄 🖤 "

"Think of your heart as a cozy blanket fort – it's a sanctuary deserving of all the cuddles and laughter of love and happiness! 🏰 🖤 "

"You deserve love and happiness as much as a sea turtle deserves a calm ocean and sandy beaches! 🐢 🏖️ "

"Your worth is like a rainbow – it stretches across the sky, reminding you that you're deserving of love and happiness every day! 🌈 🖤 "

"Your heart is like a carnival – enjoy all the love and happiness rides and cotton candy! 🎡 🖤 "

"You're as deserving of love and happiness as a panda is of bamboo and sleepy cuddles! 🐼 🌿 "

"Think of your worth as a sparkler – it lights up your life, deserving of all the dazzle and delight of love and happiness! 🎇 🤍"

"Your worth is like a cozy fireplace – it's deserving of all the warmth and crackling joy of love and happiness! 🔥 🤍"

"Your heart is like a treasure chest – full of deserving love and happiness gems to cherish! 💎 🤍"

"You deserve love and happiness as much as a kangaroo deserves a comfy pouch and playful hops! 🦘 🏠"

"Your worth is like a lucky charm – it brings you deserving love and happiness like a pot of gold at the end of the rainbow! 🍀 🌈"

"Think of your heart as a carousel – enjoy all the love and happiness horses and merry-go-round music! 🎠 🤍"

"You're as deserving of love and happiness as a sea lion is of sunbathing and a splash

in the ocean! 🌞 🌊"

"Your worth is like a warm cup of tea – it's deserving of all the coziness and serenity of love and happiness! 🍵 🤍"

"Your heart is like a garden – cultivate it with deserving love and happiness, and watch joy bloom! 🪴🌼"

"You deserve love and happiness as much as a lion deserves its mane and the courage to roar! 🦁💥"

"Your worth is like a pot of gold at the end of the rainbow – it's deserving of all the treasures of love and happiness! 🧲💰"

"Think of your heart as a playground – have fun with deserving love and happiness on the swings and slides! "

"Your worth is like a lucky star – it guides you to deserving love and happiness on every journey! 💥🤍"

"You're as deserving of love and happiness as a squirrel is of acorns and treehouse adventures! 🐿️🌳"

"Your heart is like a dance floor – deserving of all the groovy moves and rhythm of love and happiness! 🕺🎶"

"Your worth is like a cozy campfire – it's deserving of all the stories and s'mores of love and happiness! 🔥🤍"

"Think of your heart as a spaceship – launch into the universe of deserving love and happiness! 🚀🪐"

"Your worth is like a lighthouse – it shines brightly, guiding you to the deserving shores of love and happiness! 🗺️💡"

"You deserve love and happiness as much as a penguin deserves a belly slide in the snow! 🐧❄️"

"Your heart is like a magical wand – use it to create moments of love and happiness in your life! ☐ 💜"

"Think of your worth as a star in the night sky – unique and deserving of all the wishes for love and happiness! ✏️💜"

"Your worth is like a rainbow – it stretches across the sky, reminding you that you're deserving of love and happiness every day! 🌈💜"

"Your heart is like a carnival – enjoy all the love and happiness rides and cotton candy! 🎡💜"

"You're as deserving of love and happiness as a panda is of bamboo and sleepy cuddles! 🐼🍃"

"Think of your worth as a sparkler – it lights up your life, deserving of all the dazzle and delight of love and happiness! ✨💜"

"Your worth is like a cozy fireplace – it's deserving of all the warmth and crackling joy of love and happiness! 🔥💜"

"Your heart is like a treasure chest – full of deserving love and happiness gems to cherish! 💎 🤍 "

"You deserve love and happiness as much as a kangaroo deserves a comfy pouch and playful hops! 🦘 🏠 "

"Your worth is like a lucky charm – it brings you deserving love and happiness like a pot of gold at the end of the rainbow! 🍀 🪙 "

"Think of your heart as a carousel – enjoy all the love and happiness horses and merry-go-round music! 🎠 🤍 "

"You're as deserving of love and happiness as a sea lion is of sunbathing and a splash in the ocean! 🌞 🦭 "

"Your worth is like a warm cup of tea – it's deserving of all the coziness and serenity of love and happiness! ☕ 🤍 "

"Your heart is like a garden – cultivate it with deserving love and happiness, and watch joy bloom! 🌼 🌸 "

"You deserve love and happiness as much as a lion deserves its mane and the courage to roar! 🦁 🌟 "

"Your worth is like a pot of gold at the end of the rainbow – it's deserving of all the treasures of love and happiness! 🪙 💰 "

"Think of your heart as a playground – have fun with deserving love and happiness on the swings and slides! "

"Your worth is like a lucky star – it guides you to deserving love and happiness on every journey! 🎇 🩶"

"You're as deserving of love and happiness as a squirrel is of acorns and treehouse adventures! 🐿️ 🍀"

"Your heart is like a dance floor – deserving of all the groovy moves and rhythm of love and happiness! 🕺 🎶"

"Your worth is like a cozy campfire – it's deserving of all the stories and s'mores of love and happiness! 🔥 🩶"

"Think of your heart as a spaceship – launch into the universe of deserving love and happiness! 🚀 🪐"

"Your worth is like a lighthouse – it shines brightly, guiding you to the deserving shores of love and happiness! 🗺️ 💡"

"You deserve love and happiness as much as a penguin deserves a belly slide in the snow! 🐧 ❄️"

"Your heart is like a magical wand – use it to create moments of love and happiness in your life! 🪄 🩶"

"Think of your worth as a star in the night sky – unique and deserving of all the wishes for love and happiness! 🖊️ 🤍"

"Your worth is like a rainbow – it stretches across the sky, reminding you that you're deserving of love and happiness every day! 🌈 🤍"

"Your heart is like a carnival – enjoy all the love and happiness rides and cotton candy! 🎡 🤍"

"You're as deserving of love and happiness as a panda is of bamboo and sleepy cuddles! 🐼 🌿"

"Think of your worth as a sparkler – it lights up your life, deserving of all the dazzle and delight of love and happiness! 🎇 🤍"

"Your worth is like a cozy fireplace – it's deserving of all the warmth and crackling joy of love and happiness! 🔥 🤍"

"Your heart is like a treasure chest – full of deserving love and happiness gems to cherish! 💎 🤍"

"You deserve love and happiness as much as a kangaroo deserves a comfy pouch and playful hops! 🦘 🏠"

"Your worth is like a lucky charm – it brings you deserving love and happiness like a pot of gold at the end of the rainbow! 🍀 🌈"

"Think of your heart as a carousel – enjoy all the love and happiness horses and merry-go-round music! 🎠 🖤 "

"You're as deserving of love and happiness as a sea lion is of sunbathing and a splash in the ocean! ☀️ 🌊 "

"Your worth is like a warm cup of tea – it's deserving of all the coziness and serenity of love and happiness! 🍵 🖤 "

"Your heart is like a garden – cultivate it with deserving love and happiness, and watch joy bloom! 🌼 🌼 "

"You deserve love and happiness as much as a lion deserves its mane and the courage to roar! 🦁 💥 "

"Your worth is like a pot of gold at the end of the rainbow – it's deserving of all the treasures of love and happiness! 🌈 💰 "

Chapter 7

IT'S OKAY TO SEEK SUPPORT

"Seeking support is like using a GPS for your emotions – it helps you navigate the rollercoaster of life! 🗺️ 💜 "

"Remember, even superheroes need sidekicks. Seeking support is your way of recruiting your own dream team! 🦸 🐾 "

"It's okay to seek support. Think of it as ordering your favorite comfort food for the soul! 🍞 💜 "

"Just as plants need water, your soul needs support to thrive. Water your emotions with conversation! 🌱 🗨️ "

"Seeking support is like a warm and cozy sweater for your heart – it keeps you snug and protected! 📕 💗 "

"Your emotions are like puzzle pieces. Seeking support is how you find the picture on the box! 🧩 🎨 "

"Think of seeking support as a life hack for happiness – it's the shortcut to a brighter day! 💡✨"

"It's okay to seek support. Consider it a 'daily dose of mental vitamins' for your well-being! 💊"

"Just like fine wine gets better with time, your well-being improves with support and conversation! 🍷💬"

"Seeking support is like hitting the 'Refresh' button for your emotional browser. It clears the cache of worries! 🔄🌐"

"It's okay to seek support. Imagine it as a heart-to-heart conversation with your inner cheerleader! 📣💜"

"Your emotions are like hidden treasure. Seeking support is the treasure map that guides you to happiness! 🗺️💰"

"Seeking support is like turning on the 'Good Vibes Radio' – tune in and let the positivity flow! 📻🎶"

"Think of support as the key that unlocks the door to your heart's well-being. Turn it and walk in! 🔑💜"

"It's okay to seek support. Consider it your 'mental spa day' – relax and rejuvenate your mind! 🌸💆"

"Just as you charge your phone for optimum performance, seek support to power up your emotional well-being! 🔋⚡"

"Your emotions are like ingredients. Seeking support is the recipe for a delicious life! 🔍 🍳 "

"Seeking support is like a cozy umbrella in the emotional rain – it keeps you dry and comfortable! ☂️ 🏠 "

"It's okay to seek support. Think of it as a 'mind massage' that relieves the tension of daily life! 💆 🌸 "

"Seeking support is like a 'virtual hug' for your heart – it brings warmth and comfort, even from afar! 😊 💻 "

"Seeking support is like a warm cup of tea for your soul – it soothes and comforts your spirit! 🍵 🍪 "

"Think of it as an 'emotional recipe book' – seeking support adds new flavors to your life's menu! 📖 🍳 "

"It's okay to seek support. Consider it your 'heart's helpline' – open 24/7 for your well-being needs! ☎️ 💖 "

"Just as a magician needs a magic wand, your heart sometimes needs support to create happiness! □ ✨ "

"Seeking support is like a daily dose of sunshine for your soul – it brightens your inner world! 🌼 🤍 "

"Your emotions are like fine art. Seeking support is the gallery where you display your feelings! 🎨 🏛️ "

"Think of it as a 'mental massage' – seeking support kneads away the stress and knots in your mind! 🪵❄️"

"It's okay to seek support. Consider it your 'self-love spa day' – pamper your emotions! 🧖‍♀️💜"

"Seeking support is like a cozy fireplace in your heart – it warms and comforts you on a cold day! 🔥🏠"

"Just as a plant needs sunlight to grow, your well-being needs support to flourish! 🌱🌼"

"Seeking support is like having a 'compass for your emotions' – it helps you find your way back to happiness! 🧭💜"

"Think of it as a 'soul smoothie' – seeking support blends your emotions into a refreshing concoction! 🥤🍈"

"It's okay to seek support. Imagine it as a 'soul spa' that rejuvenates your inner world! 🍃🧘"

"Just as a navigator uses the North Star, seeking support guides you toward emotional well-being! ⭐🐚"

"Seeking support is like a 'mental dance party' – groove to the rhythm of well-being and joy! 💃🎵"

"Your emotions are like precious gems. Seeking support is the jeweler that polishes and showcases them! 💎 💟 "

"Think of it as a 'love letter to yourself' – seeking support expresses your care for your own heart! 📩 💟 "

"It's okay to seek support. Consider it your 'emotional gym' – work out the knots in your mind! 💪 🌀 "

"Seeking support is like a 'heart-shaped parachute' – it gently lands you in the world of well-being! 🪂 🫂 "

"Just as a chef uses various ingredients, your well-being needs a mix of support for a delicious life! 🔍 🧂 "

"Seeking support is like a 'healing playlist' for your emotions – let the music of well-being play! 🎶 💥 "

"Think of it as a 'mental treasure hunt' – seeking support uncovers the riches of your heart! 🏴 💰 "

"It's okay to seek support. Imagine it as your 'self-love hotline' – available whenever you need it! ☎ 💚 "

"Just as a scientist needs tools for discovery, your heart needs support to explore the world of well-being! 🔬 ⚪ "

"Seeking support is like a 'warm and fuzzy blanket' for your soul – it wraps you in comfort and love! 🛏 😊 "

"Your emotions are like colors on a canvas. Seeking support is the artist's brush that creates a masterpiece of well-being! 🎨🖼️"

"Think of it as a 'well-being buffet' – seeking support offers a variety of emotional delicacies to savor! 🍽️🍷"

"It's okay to seek support. Consider it your 'stress-relief recipe' – mix well with conversation and enjoy a serving of happiness! 🍪✨"

"Seeking support is like a 'comedy show for your heart' – laugh your way to well-being! 🎤🎙️"

"Think of it as a 'mental magic show' – seeking support is the trick that turns worries into wonder! 🎩✨"

"It's okay to seek support. Imagine it as your 'emotional travel agent' – plan a journey to well-being! ✈️💜"

"Just as an explorer relies on a map, your heart can rely on support to navigate the terrain of well-being! 🗺️⛰️"

"Seeking support is like a 'warm and sunny day' for your soul – bask in the rays of positivity! 🌼🌻"

"Your emotions are like pieces of art. Seeking support is the curator who arranges them into a gallery of well-being! "

"Think of it as a 'well-being potluck' – seeking support brings the most delightful emotional dishes to share! "

"It's okay to seek support. Consider it your 'emotional spa retreat' – rejuvenate your spirit! 🌸 👸 "

"Seeking support is like a 'fireworks display for your heart' – light up the sky with joy and well-being! 🎆 🍪 "

"Just as a coach guides athletes, support guides you toward your emotional well-being goals! 🏆 🎖 "

"Think of it as a 'well-being treasure chest' – seeking support unlocks the chest of emotional riches! 🗝 🔷 "

"It's okay to seek support. Imagine it as a 'life-size emotional teddy bear' – cuddle with well-being and comfort! 🧸 💚 "

"Your emotions are like ingredients in a recipe. Seeking support is the chef who creates a masterpiece of well-being! 🍞 🍘 "

"Seeking support is like a 'magic carpet ride' for your soul – let it take you to the land of well-being! 🧞✨"

"Think of it as an 'emotional spa day' – seeking support is your ticket to relaxation and self-care! 🧖"

"Just as a gardener nurtures plants, support nurtures your emotional well-being, helping it flourish! 🌱🌼"

"Seeking support is like a 'love potion' for your heart – it stirs feelings of well-being and affection! 🖊️💗"

"Your emotions are like musical notes. Seeking support is the conductor who orchestrates a symphony of well-being! "

"It's okay to seek support. Consider it your 'emotional toolset' – equip yourself with well-being skills! 🧰🔧"

"Seeking support is like a 'well-being movie night' – choose the genre of positivity and enjoy the show! 🎬🍿"

"Think of it as a 'well-being bouquet' – seeking support is the arrangement of beautiful emotions in your life! 🌷🌷"

"It's okay to seek support. Imagine it as your 'emotional library' – read well-being books and expand your mind! "

"Seeking support is like a 'well-being ice cream parlor' – savor the flavors of happiness! 🍦🍨"

"Just as a lifeguard keeps swimmers safe, support keeps your emotional well-being secure! 🏠🛟"

"Your emotions are like puzzle pieces. Seeking support is how you complete the well-being picture! 🧩🎨"

"Think of it as a 'well-being spa vacation' – relax and rejuvenate your inner world! 🗺️🐾"

"Seeking support is like a 'well-being playground' – slide into joy, swing into happiness, and play all day! 🛝🏠"

"It's okay to seek support. Consider it your 'emotional recipe book' – try out new dishes of well-being! 📖🍽️"

"Seeking support is like a 'well-being garden' – nurture your emotional flowers and watch them bloom! 🌼🌻"

"Just as a detective unravels mysteries, support helps you uncover the secrets to well-being! 🕵️🔍"

"Think of it as a 'well-being treasure hunt' – seeking support leads you to the chest of emotional riches! 🏴‍☠️💰"

"It's okay to seek support. Imagine it as a 'mental massage' that kneads away the stress in your mind! 🧖💆"

"Seeking support is like a 'well-being menu' – choose the emotional dishes that make your heart sing! 🍽️🎶"

"Your emotions are like fine art. Seeking support is the gallery where you display your feelings! 🎨🏛️"

"Think of it as a 'love letter to yourself' – seeking support expresses your care for your own heart! 📩💜"

"It's okay to seek support. Consider it your 'emotional gym' – work out the knots in your mind! 💪🧠"

"Seeking support is like a 'heart-shaped parachute' – it gently lands you in the world of well-being! 🪂🧠"

"Just as a chef uses various ingredients, your well-being needs a mix of support for a delicious life! 🔍🧂"

"Your emotions are like precious gems. Seeking support is the jeweler that polishes and showcases them! 💎💜"

"Think of it as a 'mental massage' – seeking support kneads away the stress and knots in your mind! 🧖✨"

"It's okay to seek support. Consider it your 'stress-relief recipe' – mix well with conversation and enjoy a serving of happiness! 🍪✨"

"Seeking support is like a 'comedy show for your heart' – laugh your way to well-being! 🤣 🎤"

"Just as a navigator uses the North Star, seeking support guides you toward emotional well-being! ⭐ 🧭"

"Think of it as a 'mental magic show' – seeking support is the trick that turns worries into wonder! 🎩 ✨"

"It's okay to seek support. Imagine it as your 'emotional travel agent' – plan a journey to well-being! ✈️ ♥"

"Your emotions are like ingredients in

a recipe. Seeking support is the chef who creates a masterpiece of well-being! 🍳 🥘"

"Seeking support is like a 'magic carpet ride' for your soul – let it take you to the land of well-being! 🧞 💥"

"Think of it as an 'emotional spa day' – seeking support is your ticket to relaxation and self-care! 🌿 🐱"

"It's okay to seek support. Imagine it as a 'life-size emotional teddy bear' – cuddle with well-being and comfort! 🧸 ♥"

"Just as a gardener nurtures plants, support nurtures your emotional well-being, helping it flourish! 🌱 🌼"

"Seeking support is like a 'love potion' for your heart – it stirs feelings of well-being and affection! "

"Your emotions are like musical notes. Seeking support is the conductor who orchestrates a symphony of well-being! "

Chapter 8

FORGIVENESS IS POWERFUL

"I release the weight of resentment, making room for the lightness of forgiveness. 🪦🗝️"

"With forgiveness, my heart finds solace, and I grant myself the gift of healing. 🕊️🤍"

"I free myself from the chains of grudges, embracing the liberation of forgiveness. 🧱🔑"

"Forgiveness is my bridge to peace, spanning the river of heartbreak. 🌉🌊"

"Like a phoenix, I rise from the ashes of resentment, embracing the flames of forgiveness. 🦅🔥"

"With forgiveness, I untangle the knots of anger, allowing love to flow freely. 💬🤍"

"I release the past's grip on my heart, welcoming a future illuminated by forgiveness. 🪦🎆"

"Forgiveness is the mirror where self-compassion reflects a heart full of love. ▢ 💚"

"I offer myself and others the precious gift of forgiveness, wrapped in the ribbon of grace. 🎁 💐"

"Like a gardener, I tend to the soil of my heart, nurturing forgiveness to bloom. 🌱 🌸"

"I break the chains of anger, setting my heart free to dance with the rhythms of forgiveness. ⛓ 💃"

"Forgiveness is the lighthouse guiding me through the stormy waters of heartbreak. 🏠 ⚓"

"I release the old, inviting the new, like a book of forgiveness with endless pages of love. 📚 💚"

"With forgiveness, I melt the icy grip of resentment, warming my heart with love. ❄ 🌼"

"Like a painter, I color my canvas with the vibrant shades of forgiveness, creating a masterpiece of love. 🎨 🖼"

"I unburden my heart from the heavy backpack of grudges, embracing the lightness of forgiveness. 🎒 🕊"

"Forgiveness is the key to unlocking the treasure chest of love buried beneath heartbreak. 🔑 💝"

85

"I mend the torn fabric of my heart with the threads of forgiveness, stitching love into every seam. □ ♡ "

"With forgiveness, I rewrite the story of heartbreak, turning its pages into a novel of love and redemption. ▢ ✴ "

"Like a chef, I cook up forgiveness, seasoning it with love and serving it with a side of compassion. ◍ ⌷ "

"I demolish the walls of resentment, building bridges of understanding and love. ⚒ ⛩ "

"Forgiveness is my compass, steering me away from the stormy seas of anger toward the calm waters of love. ◑ ⮌ "

"I scrub away the stains of resentment, revealing the polished surface of forgiveness beneath. ◌ ✿ "

"With forgiveness, I plant the seeds of love in the garden of my heart, nurturing their growth. □ ♥ "

"I release the grip of resentment, allowing my heart to soar like a kite in the skies of forgiveness. ◣ ✲ "

"Forgiveness is the bridge that leads me out of the darkness of heartbreak towards the dawn of love. ▦ ⛰ "

"I untangle the webs of anger, spinning them into the threads of forgiveness that weave a tapestry of love. ✸ □ "

"With forgiveness, I unlock the door to a room filled with love, leaving resentment behind. 🚪🤍"

"Like a gardener, I tend to the delicate blooms of forgiveness, nurturing a garden of love. 🌼🌷"

"I tear down the walls of resentment, constructing a bridge to love and understanding. 🏗️🌉"

"Think of forgiveness as 'rescuing your heart' from the quicksand of resentment! 🧗🫳"

"Forgiving is like 'flipping the switch' to turn off the resentment power and illuminate happiness! 💡🎇"

"Forgiveness is like a 'heart treasure map' – it guides you to the buried well-being beneath resentment! 🗺️💗"

"Consider forgiveness your 'emotional detox' – it flushes resentment toxins from your system! 💧🧖"

"Forgiveness is your 'emotional superglue' – it mends the cracks resentment left in your heart! 🩹🤍"

"Think of forgiveness as a 'ticket to a comedy show' – laugh away resentment and enjoy the performance of joy! 🎭😄"

"Forgiving is like a 'raincheck for happiness' – cash it in after you've canceled your resentment reservations! 🎟️🌼"

"Forgiveness is your 'emotional yoga' – stretch and release the tension of resentment in your heart! 🧘🤸"

"Just as a chef seasons a dish, forgiveness adds flavor to your life, removing the bitterness of resentment! 🥄🍳"

"Forgiveness is like a 'magic potion' for your heart – it turns resentment into love and well-being! 🪄💗"

"Think of forgiveness as a 'mental sunblock' – it shields your heart from the harmful rays of resentment! 🧴🌞"

"Forgiving is like a 'heart wardrobe change' – swap the heavy resentment outfit for a light, joyful one! 👗🌼"

"Forgiveness is the 'emotional trampoline' that helps you bounce back from the dive into resentment! ⬜🤸"

"Consider forgiveness your 'emotional GPS' – it reroutes you away from the traffic jam of resentment! 🗺️🚗"

"Forgiveness is your 'emotional passport' – it allows you to travel freely without carrying resentment baggage! 🧳⚫"

"Think of forgiveness as a 'happy heart dance party' – let go of resentment and groove to the rhythm of joy! 💃🎶"

"Forgiving is like a 'heart garden' – pull out the weeds of resentment and cultivate a beautiful bed of well-being flowers! 🏵️ 🌱"

"Forgiveness is your 'emotional deflector shield' – it keeps resentment missiles from hitting your heart! 🛡️ 💜"

"Just as a lifeguard watches over swimmers, forgiveness watches over your emotional waters, keeping them resentment-free! 🏠 🏠"

"Think of forgiveness as 'peaceful meditation' for your heart – it calms the storm of resentment within! 🧘 ☁️"

"Forgiveness is like a 'heart-shaped magnet' – it attracts well-being and repels resentment! 🧲 💔"

"Consider forgiveness your 'heart's reset button' – press it to clear the slate of resentment and start fresh! ⚪ 📑"

"Forgiving is like a 'heart orchestra' – it harmonizes your emotions and composes a symphony of well-being! 🎻 🎵"

"Forgiveness is the 'emotional backpack' that lightens the load of resentment as you journey through life! 🎒 🧗"

"Think of forgiveness as 'mental floss' – it helps clean out the stuck bits of resentment between your thoughts! ⬜ 🧹"

"Forgiveness is your 'emotional sunshine' – it melts away the icy resentment and warms your heart with joy! 🌞 🤍 "

"Just as a sculptor shapes clay, forgiveness molds your heart by removing the excess resentment! 🗿🪨 "

"Consider forgiveness your 'emotional first aid kit' – apply it to soothe the wounds of resentment! 🩹🧰 "

"Forgiveness is like a 'soul yoga session' – stretch out the resentment knots and find emotional flexibility! 🧘💪 "

"Think of forgiveness as a 'magic wand' for your soul – it transforms resentment into kindness and well-being! 🪄 💗 "

"Forgiving is like 'airing out your heart' – let the breeze of forgiveness clear away the stuffiness of resentment! 🫴🫁 "

"Forgiveness is your 'emotional life preserver' – it keeps you afloat and safe from the waves of resentment! 🛟🌊 "

"Consider forgiveness your 'heart's art studio' – create a masterpiece of well-being by painting over the canvas of resentment! 🎨🖼️ "

"Forgiveness is like a 'mental eraser' – it rubs out resentment scribbles and makes space for happiness doodles! 🧽📝 "

"Think of forgiveness as 'emotional sunblock' – it protects your heart from the harsh UV rays of resentment! 🧴 🌞 "

"Forgiving is like a 'heart scavenger hunt' – seek out the hidden treasures of well-being by uncovering resentment! 🔍 🎁 "

"Forgiveness is your 'emotional superhero shield' – it deflects the resentment arrows and keeps your heart safe! 🦸 🛡️ "

"Consider forgiveness your 'soul's spring cleaning' – sweep out resentment dust bunnies and let joy sparkle! 🧹 ✨ "

"Forgiveness is like a 'heart-powered vacuum' – it sucks up the emotional dirt of resentment, leaving a clean, happy heart! ⬜ 🏠 "

"Think of forgiveness as a 'happy heart dance-off' – let go of resentment and groove to the rhythm of joy! 🕺 🎶 "

"Forgiving is like 'air conditioning for the heart' – it cools down the fiery resentment and brings a refreshing breeze of well-being! ❄️ 🔌 "

"Forgiveness is your 'emotional squeegee' – it wipes away the residue of resentment, revealing a clear view of happiness! 🪨 ⬜ "

"Consider forgiveness your 'heart's dream catcher' – it snags the negative dreams of resentment and allows only the good ones to pass through! 🌙☐ "

"Forgiveness is like a 'mental paintbrush' – use it to create a beautiful masterpiece of well-being by covering over resentment stains! 🖌🎨 "

"Think of forgiveness as 'emotional acupuncture' – it releases the blocked energy of resentment and restores emotional balance! 🗝✨ "

"Forgiving is like a 'soul GPS' – it reroutes you away from the emotional traffic jam of resentment and guides you towards well-being! 🗺🚗 "

"Forgiveness is your 'emotional trampoline' – it helps you bounce back from the dive into resentment and leap towards happiness! ☐ 🏔 "

"Consider forgiveness your 'heart's reset button' – press it to clear the slate of resentment and start fresh with a heart full of well-being! ⚪🗒 "

"Forgiveness is like a 'heart orchestra' – it harmonizes your emotions and composes a symphony of well-being that will make your heart sing with joy! 🎻🎵 "

"Think of forgiveness as a 'soulful exfoliation' – scrub away resentment to reveal your inner glow! 🧖🕊️"

"Forgiving is like a 'mental magic potion' – it transforms resentment into a sparkling elixir of well-being! ☐ 💖"

"Forgiveness is your 'emotional sunscreen' – it shields your heart from the harmful rays of resentment! 🧴☀️"

"Consider forgiveness your 'heart's peace treaty' – a truce with resentment, signed in favor of happiness and well-being! 🕊️📜"

"Forgiveness is like 'rescuing your heart' from the quicksand of resentment! 🧗🌊"

"Forgiving is like 'flipping the switch' to turn off the resentment power and illuminate happiness! 💡🎆"

"Forgiveness is like a 'heart treasure map' – it guides you to the buried well-being beneath resentment! 🗺️💖"

"Consider forgiveness your 'emotional detox' – it flushes resentment toxins from your system, leaving only the refreshing flow of well-being! 💧🧘"

"Forgiving is your 'emotional superglue' – it mends the cracks resentment left in your heart, making it whole again with well-being! ✏️💚"

"Think of forgiveness as a 'happy heart dance party' – let go of resentment and dance to the rhythm of joy! 🧘🎶"

"Forgiveness is like a 'heart wardrobe change' – swap the heavy resentment outfit for a light, joyful one! 👗🌼"

"Consider forgiveness your 'emotional first aid kit' – apply it to soothe the wounds of resentment and tend to your heart's well-being! 🩹📱"

"Forgiving is like 'airing out your heart' – let the breeze of forgiveness clear away the stuffiness of resentment and invite in the fresh air of well-being! 🫳👊"

"Forgiveness is your 'emotional sunshine' – it melts away the icy resentment and warms your heart with the rays of joy and well-being! 🌼♡"

"As a composer, I craft melodies of reconciliation where forgiveness takes the lead, and love sets the rhythm. 🎵♥
"

"Forgiving is like 'air conditioning for the heart' – it cools down the fiery resentment and brings a refreshing breeze of well-being! ❄️👊"

"Forgiveness is like a 'mental eraser' – it rubs out resentment scribbles and makes space for happiness doodles! ⬜📝"

94

"Consider forgiveness your 'heart's art studio' – create a masterpiece of well-being by painting over the canvas of resentment! 🎨✨"

"Forgiveness is your 'emotional deflector shield' – it keeps resentment missiles from hitting your heart and allows well-being to be your protective armor! 🛡️💜"

Chapter 9

I CAN LEARN AND GROW

"I'm like a 'knowledge sponge' – soaking up wisdom from every experience and growing wiser! "

"Every situation is a 'life classroom' – I'm the eager student, ready to ace the test of personal growth! "

"I can turn any experience into 'life fertilizer' – watch me grow and bloom from the lessons I've sown! "

"I'm on the 'personal growth express' – choo-chooing through life's lessons and getting smarter with every stop! "

"I see life as a 'learning buffet' – I'll taste a bit of everything and come back with a full plate of wisdom! "

"Every experience is a 'growth smoothie' – blending together challenges and lessons, and sipping on self-improvement! "

"I'm a 'personal growth scientist' – experimenting with life's lessons and concocting a formula for success! 🧑‍🔬🖊️"

"I can learn and grow, just like a plant reaching for the sun – except I'm reaching for knowledge and self-improvement! 🌱🌼"

"Life is a 'personal growth adventure' – I'm the intrepid explorer, discovering treasures of wisdom at every turn! ⚫🗺️"

"I view challenges as 'personal growth puzzles' – I'll solve them and unlock the wisdom within! 🧩📚"

"I'm a 'knowledge butterfly' – transforming from a caterpillar of ignorance into a butterfly of wisdom! 🐛🦋"

"Every experience is a 'learning game' – I'm leveling up in life, and my high score is personal growth! 🎮🏆"

"I can learn and grow, like a 'life gardener' – I tend to the seeds of knowledge and watch the flowers of wisdom bloom! 🌱🌺"

"I'm on a 'personal growth rollercoaster' – holding on tight as I twist, turn, and learn from life's thrilling ride! 📔📚"

"I see life as a 'growth buffet' – I'll take a little bit of adversity and a heaping plate of wisdom, please! 🍽️🍽️"

"Every situation is a 'personal growth recipe' – I'm the master chef, cooking up wisdom with every experience! 🔍💭"

"I release the weight of resentment, making room for the lightness of forgiveness. 🔒🗝️"

"With forgiveness, my heart finds solace, and I grant myself the gift of healing. 🕊️🤍"

"I free myself from the chains of grudges, embracing the liberation of forgiveness. 🔗🗝️"

"Forgiveness is my bridge to peace, spanning the river of heartbreak. 🌉✋"

"Like a phoenix, I rise from the ashes of resentment, embracing the flames of forgiveness. 🦅🔥"

"With forgiveness, I untangle the knots of anger, allowing love to flow freely. 🪢🤍"

"I release the past's grip on my heart, welcoming a future illuminated by forgiveness. 🕯️✨"

"Forgiveness is the mirror where self-compassion reflects a heart full of love. ☐ 🖤"

"I offer myself and others the precious gift of forgiveness, wrapped in the ribbon of grace. 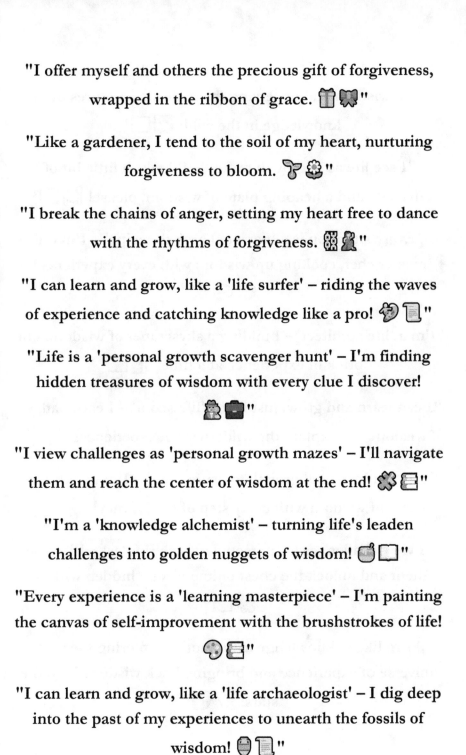"

"Like a gardener, I tend to the soil of my heart, nurturing forgiveness to bloom. "

"I break the chains of anger, setting my heart free to dance with the rhythms of forgiveness. "

"I can learn and grow, like a 'life surfer' – riding the waves of experience and catching knowledge like a pro! "

"Life is a 'personal growth scavenger hunt' – I'm finding hidden treasures of wisdom with every clue I discover! "

"I view challenges as 'personal growth mazes' – I'll navigate them and reach the center of wisdom at the end! "

"I'm a 'knowledge alchemist' – turning life's leaden challenges into golden nuggets of wisdom! "

"Every experience is a 'learning masterpiece' – I'm painting the canvas of self-improvement with the brushstrokes of life! "

"I can learn and grow, like a 'life archaeologist' – I dig deep into the past of my experiences to unearth the fossils of wisdom! "

"I'm on a 'personal growth safari' – tracking the footprints of wisdom and observing the majestic creatures of knowledge in the wild! 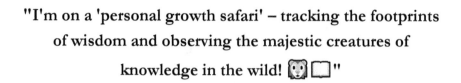"

"I see life as a 'growth buffet' – I'll take a little bit of adversity and a heaping plate of wisdom, please! "

"Every situation is a 'personal growth recipe' – I'm the master chef, cooking up wisdom with every experience! 🔍🍪"

"I'm a 'life architect' – building a skyscraper of wisdom, one brick of experience at a time! 🏫📖"

"I can learn and grow, just like a 'life scout' – I earn badges of wisdom as I explore the wilderness of experience! ⛰️📒"

"Life is a 'personal growth treasure hunt' – I'm unearthing gems of wisdom with every step of the journey! 🔷🗺️"

"I view challenges as 'personal growth riddles' – I'll solve them and unlock the chest of knowledge hidden within! "

"I'm like a 'knowledge astronaut' – exploring the vast universe of experience and bringing back wisdom from the stars! 🚀🪐"

"Every experience is a 'learning tapestry' – I'm weaving a masterpiece of wisdom with threads of life's ups and downs! 🧵📖"

. "I can learn and grow, like a 'life detective' – I uncover clues to self-improvement in every case I encounter! 🕵️📖"

"I'm on a 'personal growth road trip' – cruising through life's lessons, collecting souvenirs of wisdom along the way! 🚗🏠"

"I see life as a 'growth smorgasbord' – I'll sample a bit of everything and savor the flavors of knowledge! 🍽️📖"

"Every situation is a 'personal growth mosaic' – I'm piecing together a beautiful picture of wisdom, one experience at a time! ✳️📖"

"I'm a 'knowledge blacksmith' – forging wisdom from the fires of life's challenges and hammering out self-improvement! ⚒️📖"

"I can learn and grow, like a 'life surfer' – riding the waves of experience and catching knowledge like a pro! 🌊📜"

"Life is a 'personal growth scavenger hunt' – I'm finding hidden treasures of wisdom with every clue I discover! 🧸💼"

"I view challenges as 'personal growth mazes' – I'll navigate them and reach the center of wisdom at the end! 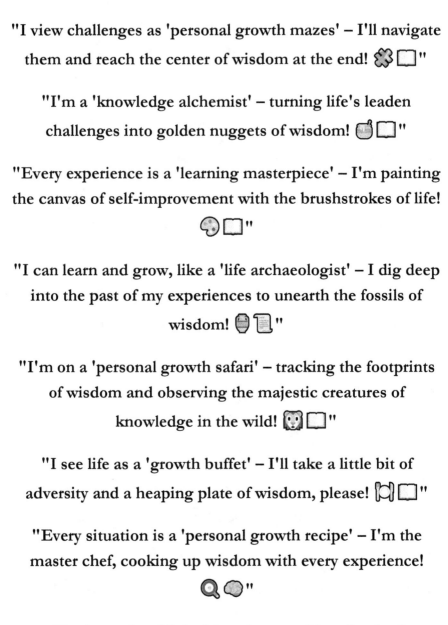"

"I'm a 'knowledge alchemist' – turning life's leaden challenges into golden nuggets of wisdom! "

"Every experience is a 'learning masterpiece' – I'm painting the canvas of self-improvement with the brushstrokes of life! "

"I can learn and grow, like a 'life archaeologist' – I dig deep into the past of my experiences to unearth the fossils of wisdom! "

"I'm on a 'personal growth safari' – tracking the footprints of wisdom and observing the majestic creatures of knowledge in the wild! "

"I see life as a 'growth buffet' – I'll take a little bit of adversity and a heaping plate of wisdom, please! "

"Every situation is a 'personal growth recipe' – I'm the master chef, cooking up wisdom with every experience! "

"I release the old, inviting the new, like a book of forgiveness with endless pages of love. "

"With forgiveness, I melt the icy grip of resentment, warming my heart with love. ❄️☀️"

"Like a painter, I color my canvas with the vibrant shades of forgiveness, creating a masterpiece of love. 🎨🖼️"

"I unburden my heart from the heavy backpack of grudges, embracing the lightness of forgiveness. 🎒💗"

"Forgiveness is the key to unlocking the treasure chest of love buried beneath heartbreak. 🗝️💜"

"I mend the torn fabric of my heart with the threads of forgiveness, stitching love into every seam. ⬜ ♥️"

"With forgiveness, I rewrite the story of heartbreak, turning its pages into a novel of love and redemption. 📖✳️"

"Like a chef, I cook up forgiveness, seasoning it with love and serving it with a side of compassion. 🔍🍽️"

"I demolish the walls of resentment, building bridges of understanding and love. 🚧🏰"

"Forgiveness is my compass, steering me away from the stormy seas of anger toward the calm waters of love. 🧭⛵"

"I scrub away the stains of resentment, revealing the polished surface of forgiveness beneath. 🧽✨"

"With forgiveness, I plant the seeds of love in the garden of my heart, nurturing their growth. □ 🤍"

"Like a sculptor, I carve forgiveness from the stone of heartbreak, revealing the masterpiece of love within. □ ✏️"

"I release the grip of resentment, allowing my heart to soar like a kite in the skies of forgiveness. 🪁💥"

"Forgiveness is the bridge that leads me out of the darkness of heartbreak towards the dawn of love. 🏙️🌅"

"I untangle the webs of anger, spinning them into the threads of forgiveness that weave a tapestry of love. 🕸️□"

"With forgiveness, I unlock the door to a room filled with love, leaving resentment behind. 🚪🤍"

"Like a gardener, I tend to the delicate blooms of forgiveness, nurturing a garden of love. 💮🌷"

"I tear down the walls of resentment, constructing a bridge to love and understanding. 🏗️🏛️"

"I'm a 'life architect' – building a skyscraper of wisdom, one brick of experience at a time! 🏗️📖"

"I can learn and grow, just like a 'life scout' – I earn badges of wisdom as I explore the wilderness of experience! ⛰️📜"

"Life is a 'personal growth treasure hunt' – I'm unearthing gems of wisdom with every step of the journey! 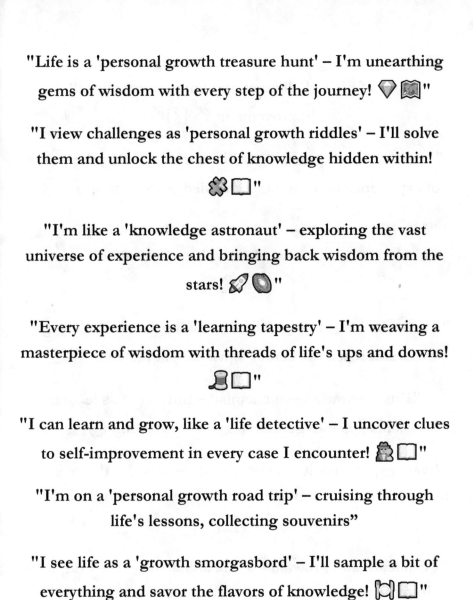 "

"I view challenges as 'personal growth riddles' – I'll solve them and unlock the chest of knowledge hidden within! "

"I'm like a 'knowledge astronaut' – exploring the vast universe of experience and bringing back wisdom from the stars! "

"Every experience is a 'learning tapestry' – I'm weaving a masterpiece of wisdom with threads of life's ups and downs! "

"I can learn and grow, like a 'life detective' – I uncover clues to self-improvement in every case I encounter! "

"I'm on a 'personal growth road trip' – cruising through life's lessons, collecting souvenirs"

"I see life as a 'growth smorgasbord' – I'll sample a bit of everything and savor the flavors of knowledge! "

"Every situation is a 'personal growth mosaic' – I'm piecing together a beautiful picture of wisdom, one experience at a time! "

"I'm a 'knowledge blacksmith' – forging wisdom from the fires of life's challenges and hammering out self-improvement! ⚒📖"

"I can learn and grow, like a 'life surfer' – riding the waves of experience and catching knowledge like a pro! 🏄📜"

"Life is a 'personal growth scavenger hunt' – I'm finding hidden treasures of wisdom with every clue I discover! 🕵️💼"

"I view challenges as 'personal growth mazes' – I'll navigate them and reach the center of wisdom at the end! 🧩📖"

"I'm a 'knowledge alchemist' – turning life's leaden challenges into golden nuggets of wisdom! 👍📖"

"Every experience is a 'learning masterpiece' – I'm painting the canvas of self-improvement with the brushstrokes of life! 🎨📖"

"I can learn and grow, like a 'life archaeologist' – I dig deep into the past of my experiences to unearth the fossils of wisdom! 🗿📜"

"I'm on a 'personal growth safari' – tracking the footprints of wisdom and observing the majestic creatures of knowledge in the wild! 🐨📖"

"I see life as a 'growth buffet' – I'll take a little bit of adversity and a heaping plate of wisdom, please! 🖐️📖"

"Every situation is a 'personal growth recipe' – I'm the master chef, cooking up wisdom with every experience! 🔍🍳"

"I'm a 'life architect' – building a skyscraper of wisdom, one brick of experience at a time! 🏗️📖"

"I can learn and grow, just like a 'life scout' – I earn badges of wisdom as I explore the wilderness of experience! ⛰️📋"

"Life is a 'personal growth treasure hunt' – I'm unearthing gems of wisdom with every step of the journey! 💎🗺️"

"I view challenges as 'personal growth riddles' – I'll solve them and unlock the chest of knowledge hidden within! ✳️📖"

Chapter 10

I HAVE HOPE FOR THE FUTURE

"I'm like a 'hopeful heart gardener' – planting seeds of optimism that will bloom into a garden of love and happiness! 🌷🌷"

"I believe in 'relationship karma' – the more hope I sow, the more love and happiness I'll reap! 🌿💗"

"I'm the 'love and happiness magnet' – attracting them with my positive hope vibes! 🧲💙"

"I see hope as my 'heart's GPS' – guiding me to the destination of love and happiness! 🗺️💗"

"I'm the 'optimism chef' – cooking up a future full of love and happiness with a dash of hope! 🍳🍽️"

"Hope is my 'emotional superpower' – with it, I can conquer any relationship challenge! 💪💙"

"I'm like a 'hopeful love explorer' – navigating the uncharted waters of the heart, seeking hidden treasures of joy! ⛰️ 💎 "

"I believe in 'heart's resilience' – it can bounce back from anything, with hope as the trampoline! 🗨️ 💚 "

"I'm the 'hopeful stargazer' – looking up at the sky, knowing that love and happiness are my destiny among the stars! 🌑 ☆ "

"I keep my heart as open as a 'hope-filled book' – ready to write new chapters of love and happiness! 📖 💚 "

"I'm a 'hopeful architect' – designing a blueprint for a love-filled and happiness-infused future! 🏢 🏠 "

"Hope is my 'emotional fuel' – it keeps the engine of my heart running toward the horizon of love and happiness! 🔋 💚 "

"I'm the 'hopeful artist' – painting a masterpiece of love and happiness with every brushstroke of optimism! 🎨 💚 "

"I believe in 'love and happiness constellations' – there are stars of hope lighting up my future! ✨ 💜 "

"I'm like a 'hopeful heart gardener' – nurturing the soil of my soul so love and happiness can flourish! 🔑 🌼 "

"I see hope as my 'emotional compass' – it always points me in the direction of love and happiness! 🧭 💜"

"I'm the 'optimism magician' – turning hope into a bouquet of love and a box of happiness tricks! ☐ 🎩"

"I believe in 'relationship rebirth' – from the ashes of the past, the phoenix of hope rises! 🕊 💜"

"May hope be the North Star guiding my ship to the shores of love and happiness. 🗡 "

"I'm launching my heart into the cosmos of possibilities, where love and joy are the brightest constellations. 🚀"

"Sailing through life's rivers, my heart is set on discovering the hidden treasures of love and happiness. 📫"

"With each sunrise, my optimism blooms like a field of wildflowers, paving the way for love and laughter. 🔒"

"I am the champion of hope, standing on the winner's podium with love and happiness as my prized trophies. 🏆 "

"I'm the captain of my own destiny, navigating life's waves with hope as my compass, guiding me to love's harbor. 🐚"

"Planting the seeds of hope in the soil of my heart, I watch them grow into the sturdy trees of love and the shade of happiness. 🍀"

"Life is a kite, and I'm soaring high with the string of hope, flying towards the boundless skies of love and laughter. 🪁"

"Just like a tree in the autumn, I let go of the past to make space for the colorful leaves of love and happiness in my future. 🍂"

"My life's a grand stage where hope takes the spotlight, and love and laughter are the stars of my performance. 🎭"

"I'm an archer of dreams, aiming my arrow of hope at the target of love, with joy as the bullseye. 🎯"

"Life's a symphony, and I compose my own melodies with hope as the conductor, orchestrating the harmonies of love and happiness. 🎵"

"In the city of life, I'm building bridges of hope that lead me to the skyscrapers of love and the bustling streets of laughter. 🏙️"

"I'm flying high on the helicopter of optimism, surveying the landscape for the hidden treasures of love and joy. 🚁 "

"Cycling through the journey of life, hope is my trusty bike, taking me down the scenic routes to love and happiness. 🚲"

"I'm an astronaut of the heart, exploring the uncharted space of possibilities, with love and happiness as my cosmic discoveries. 🌑"

"Every day is a balloon filled with hope, lifting my spirits and carrying me towards the skies of love and laughter. 🎈"

"Life is a cocktail party, and hope is my favorite drink, served with a garnish of love and a splash of happiness. 🍸"

"I'm on a never-ending train ride through life, with hope as my locomotive, pulling me toward the stations of love and laughter. 🚂"

"I'm driving the truck of determination, transporting my cargo of hope to the warehouses of love and happiness. 🚚"

"Just like a sunflower, I turn my face towards the sun of hope, and its warmth nurtures the love and happiness in my heart. 🌼"

"Each day is a new canvas, and I paint it with strokes of hope, creating masterpieces filled with love and joy. 🖼️"

"Life is an ice cream parlor, and I'm savoring the scoops of hope, topped with swirls of love and sprinkles of happiness. 🍦"

"I'm flying the helicopter of optimism, soaring above the clouds, with love and joy as my destination. 🚁"

"I'm a magician of the heart, conjuring hope into reality, where love and laughter are my greatest tricks. ☐"

"Embrace the future with open arms, for it's a treasure chest filled with love and happiness waiting to be discovered! "

"Like a squirrel with an acorn, I'm storing hope for a brighter tomorrow, where love and laughter bloom like wildflowers! 🐿️🌻"

"I'm the captain of my hope ship, sailing through the sea of life, seeking the hidden islands of love and happiness! "

"In the story of my life, every chapter is a surprise plot twist, and I believe the next one will be full of love and joy! 📖🤍"

"Today's hope is tomorrow's love, and with each sunrise, I'm one step closer to my next burst of happiness! 🔒😀"

"I'm a hope-fueled rocket, launching into the universe of possibility, where love and laughter are the stars of my destiny! 🚀 🖊 "

"My heart is an eternal optimist, knowing that even in the darkest night, there's a glimmer of dawn and a promise of love and joy! ♥ 🔔 "

"Just like a curious cat, I'm exploring the unknown, ready to pounce on the surprises life has in store, like love and delight! 🐱 🎁 "

"I'm a hope gardener, sowing seeds of optimism and tending to my heart's soil, knowing that love and happiness will bloom in due time! 🌱 ☁ "

"I'm like a kid in a candy store of hope, excitedly picking out sweet moments of love and happiness, one day at a time! 🍭 ☺ "

"Life's a puzzle, and every piece of hope I find brings me closer to revealing the beautiful picture of love and joy! ♥ "

"My heart is a hopeful compass, always pointing towards the direction of love and happiness, guiding me through life's maze! ♥ "

"I'm an eternal optimist, believing that in the library of life, there are countless unwritten chapters filled with love and laughter! 📚😄"

"Like a magician with a never-ending hat, I keep pulling hope out of my heart, and with it, I conjure love and happiness! 🎩✨"

"Every day is a new chance to unwrap the gift of hope, and inside it, I find the treasures of love and joy! 🎁💜"

"I'm a hope miner, digging deep into the caverns of life, knowing that the gems of love and laughter are hidden just beneath the surface! ⛏️💎"

"In the orchestra of life, I play the hopeful tune, believing that love and happiness will be the symphony of my future! 🎶"

"Just like a kite in the wind, I'm soaring on the currents of hope, reaching for the skies where love and joy await! "

"My heart's a culinary artist, crafting a recipe of hope, with a dash of love and a heap of happiness, ready to serve it to the world! 🔍💜"

"I'm a hope scientist, conducting experiments in life's laboratory, confident that the formula for love and laughter is within reach! 🧑‍🔬💥"

"Life's a treasure hunt, and every step I take is a clue leading me closer to the chest of love and happiness at the end! 🏴‍☠️🏆"

"My soul is a poet, composing verses of hope, where the stanzas are filled with the sweet words of love and joy! 📝💚"

"I'm a hope collector, amassing moments of optimism, knowing that each one is a step closer to the grand collection of love and happiness! 📄💗"

"Just like a hopeful gardener, I'm watering my dreams, tending to the soil of my heart, where the seeds of love and happiness are sprouting! 🌾🔑"

"I'm a hope DJ, spinning tunes of positivity, and I'm convinced the next track will be a hit, filled with love and pure happiness! 🎧🎵"

"I'm the 'hopeful captain' of my heart's ship – sailing the seas of love and happiness with a hopeful breeze! ⛵💚"

"I keep my heart as open as a 'hope-filled door' – welcoming love and happiness into my life! 🚪💚"

"I'm a 'hopeful navigator' – charting a course for a future filled with love and happiness! 🗺️💟 "

"Hope is my 'emotional sunshine' – it warms my heart and makes love and happiness grow! 🌼 🤍 "

"I'm like a 'hopeful love architect' – designing a love blueprint for a happiness foundation! 🏗️🏠 "

"I believe in 'love and happiness constellations' – there are stars of hope lighting up my future! ✨ 💟 "

"Like a joy-seeking missile, I'm locked onto the target of happiness, and my warhead is hope! 🚀 🎯 "

"I see hope as my 'emotional compass' – it always points me in the direction of love and happiness! 🧭 🤍 "

"I'm the 'optimism magician' – turning hope into a bouquet of love and a box of happiness tricks! □ 💐 "

"I believe in 'relationship rebirth' – from the ashes of the past, the phoenix of hope rises! 🐦 🤍 "

"I'm the 'hopeful captain' of my heart's ship – sailing the seas of love and happiness with a hopeful breeze! ⛵ 🤍 "

"I keep my heart as open as a 'hope-filled door' – welcoming love and happiness into my life! 🚪 🤍 "

"I'm a 'hopeful navigator' – charting a course for a future filled with love and happiness! 🗺️💗"

"Hope is my 'emotional sunshine' – it warms my heart and makes love and happiness grow! 🌞💗"

"I'm like a 'hopeful love architect' – designing a love blueprint for a happiness foundation! 🏫🏠"

"I believe in 'love and happiness constellations' – there are stars of hope lighting up my future! ✨💗"

"I see hope as my 'emotional compass' – it always points me in the direction of love and happiness! 🧭💗"

"I'm the 'optimism magician' – turning hope into a bouquet of love and a box of happiness tricks! □ 💐"

"I believe in 'relationship rebirth' – from the ashes of the past, the phoenix of hope rises! 🕊️💗"

"I'm the 'hopeful captain' of my heart's ship – sailing the seas of love and happiness with a hopeful breeze! ⛵💗"

"I keep my heart as open as a 'hope-filled door' – welcoming love and happiness into my life! 🚪💗"

"I'm a 'hopeful navigator' – charting a course for a future filled with love and happiness! 🗺️💗"

"Hope is my 'emotional sunshine' – it warms my heart and makes love and happiness grow! 🌼 🤍"

"I'm like a 'hopeful love architect' – designing a love blueprint for a happiness foundation! 📋 🏠"

"I believe in 'love and happiness constellations' – there are stars of hope lighting

up my future! ✨ 🖤"

"I see hope as my 'emotional compass' – it always points me in the direction of love and happiness! 🧭 🤍"

"I'm the 'optimism magician' – turning hope into a bouquet of love and a box of happiness tricks! ☐ 🏵"

"I believe in 'relationship rebirth' – from the ashes of the past, the phoenix of hope rises! 🕊 🤍"

"I'm the 'hopeful captain' of my heart's ship – sailing the seas of love and happiness with a hopeful breeze! ⛵ 🤍"

"I keep my heart as open as a 'hope-filled door' – welcoming love and happiness into my life! 🚪 🤍"

"I'm a 'hopeful navigator' – charting a course for a future filled with love and happiness! 🗺 🖤"

"Hope is my 'emotional sunshine' – it warms my heart and makes love and happiness grow! 🌼 🤍"

"I'm like a 'hopeful love architect' – designing a love blueprint for a happiness foundation! 🏗️ 🏠"

"I believe in 'love and happiness constellations' – there are stars of hope lighting up my future! 💫 💝"

"My heart is an open book, eager to write new chapters filled with love stories and comedic plot twists! 📖 😄"

"I see hope as my 'emotional compass' – it always points me in the direction of love and happiness! 🧭 🤍"

"I'm the 'optimism magician' – turning hope into a bouquet of love and a box of happiness tricks! ▢ 💐"

"I believe in 'relationship rebirth' – from the ashes of the past, the phoenix of hope rises! 🕊️ 🤍"

"I'm the 'hopeful captain' of my heart's ship – sailing the seas of love and happiness with a hopeful breeze! ⛵ 🤍"

"I keep my heart as open as a 'hope-filled door' – welcoming love and happiness into my life! 🚪 🤍"

NOTES

NOTES

NOTES

NOTES

NOTES

NOTES

NOTES

NOTES

NOTES

Notes

NOTES

NOTES

Thank You

A STANDING OVATION, PLEASE!

Congratulations! You've made it to the end of "The Love Letters I Never Received."

We're thrilled that you stuck with us through a rollercoaster of emotions, funny affirmations, and heartwarming moments. Now, it's time to give yourself a well-deserved round of applause!

But before you dash off to conquer the world with your newfound wisdom, let's share some laughter and gratitude:

- ❖ Thanks to you: You, yes, you! Thank you for choosing to explore this wacky, heartwarming, and occasionally absurd journey of healing with us. You're awesome!

- ❖ Affirmation Aficionados: To all the affirmation enthusiasts out there, we hope you had as much fun reading these quirky little mantras as we did creating them. Keep laughing, healing, and living your best life!

❖ Heartbreak Survivors Unite: To everyone who's been through heartbreak and lived to tell the tale – we salute you! Your strength and resilience are nothing short of amazing.

❖ Laughter Heals: A big shoutout to the power of humor. Laughter truly is the best medicine, and we hope you found plenty of chuckles within these pages.

❖ Emotional Rollercoaster: We hope your emotional rollercoaster ride was a thrilling one, with just the right amount of dips, loops, and heartwarming moments. We promise, no nausea bags required!

❖ Never Stop Learning: The world is your classroom, and every experience, even heartbreak, is a lesson. Keep growing, keep learning, and keep being amazing.

❖ Don't Forget Self-Care: You're not just a reader; you're a superstar! Remember, self-care isn't a luxury; it's a necessity. Don't forget to treat yourself like the rockstar you are.

❖ Support Squad: To all the friends, family, and therapists who lend their shoulders and ears, you're the real MVPs. Let's hear it for the support squad!

❖ Forgiveness Rules: The art of forgiveness can be as liberating as a trapeze act. Don't forget to swing freely and release those resentments.

❖ The Future Is Bright: Keep that heart open and your eyes on the horizon. The future holds love, happiness, and countless more chapters in your incredible story.

We've had an absolute blast taking you through the ups and downs of healing a broken heart with humor, inspiration, and a dash of absurdity. Now, it's time to take the world by storm and share your newfound wisdom and laughter with all those who cross your path.

You've been an incredible audience, and we're sending you all the positive vibes and laughter for your future adventures. So go on, conquer the world, and never forget that you're the star of your own love story.

With love, laughter, and a million thanks,
Your comedic healer

Sonja Cross

P.S. If you ever find yourself in need of more laughter and affirmation, you know where to find us.